Facts about
KOREA

© 1986 by Korean Overseas Information Service

First published in 1986
by Hollym Corporation; Publishers, Seoul, Korea

ISBN: 0-89346-268-3

American Edition

Heian International, Inc.
P.O. Box 1013
Union City, California 94587

86 87 88 89 90 10 9 8 7 6 5 4 3 2 1

Printed in Korea

Facts about
KOREA

PRODUCED BY
H. EDWARD KIM

HEIAN INTERNATIONAL, INC.

CONTENTS

Social Development and Quality of Life

Customs and Traditions

Arts

Religions

Sports

Tourism

Appendices

Devastated by the Korean War, Seoul has grown into one of

the world's largest metropolises with nine million people.

INTRODUCTION

The Korean peninsula extends due south of Manchuria, curving gently east and then west like the jade commas dangling from the golden crowns of its ancient kings.

This mountainous land bridge between North Asia and the outside world has always possessed great strategic importance. Invaders from the north stormed southward to mount invasions upon Japan, just a few hundred miles to the east, and both ancient and modern Japan attacked the peninsula to obtain a base for northward advances.

Yet in times of peace Korea was a cultural channel between China and the islands of Japan. Before the peninsula was united by the Shilla Kingdom in 668, the Paekche Kingdom, its contemporary, had contributed significantly to Japanese culture and knowledge. The Shilla Kingdom itself traded with nations as distant as India and Persia, as well as China. During its renascent periods Korea was an originator and repository of philosophic, religious and artistic achievements that influenced much of Asia.

Despite millennia of cultural and political ties with China, Korea maintained its individuality. Sui and Tang armies from China, the Golden Tartars, the Mongols—and others—have marched on Korean soil, only to recede like the seas on its three shores. Finally, from the end of the 16th century, Korea deliberately sought isolation, a reaction to the appalling suffering and destruction wrought by two successive Japanese invasions. Even in the 19th century, when China and Japan had been opened to the West by gunboats and per-suasion, Korea remained the "Hermit Kingdom," and was virtually unknown abroad.

The necessary transition from a self-isolated, hierar-chical society to a modern nation would have been a difficult process, even with a world of time: but time was something the world would not grant. When the slow, painful opening began late in the 19th century, Korea again became the battleground of foreign power conflicts for influence in North Asia. Russia and an expanding Japanese empire struggled for economic and political control, while China sought to maintain the traditional *status quo* of loose suzerainty. The Western powers—the United States, Britain, Germany and France—wrested such economic concessions as mineral and timber rights from the beleaguered, 500-year-old Chosŏn Kingdom.

After years of upheaval and uncertainty, the nation was annexed by Japan in 1910. A determined struggle against this foreign domination became the crucible of a modern Korean nationalism and patriotic fervor.

The joy that greeted liberation upon Japanese sur-render to the Allies at the end of World War II on August 15, 1945 was tragically short-lived. The Union of Soviet Socialist Republics and the United States agreed on a temporary division of the peninsula into northern and southern zones at the 38th parallel to accept the surrender of Japanese forces. But it soon became clear that the USSR considered the division an opportunity to inculcate the Communist creed. The gloom of colonialism was replaced by the despair of national division of one of the world's most homogeneous people when Moscow refused to allow United Nations-supervised elections in the northern zone.

Thus the Western world had little opportunity to learn about Korea before the Korean War was precipitated by a surprise attack from North Korea on June 25, 1950. The three-year war brought untold suffering to the Koreans, leaving almost the whole land devastated and more than a million killed or wounded in South Korea alone.

It was only in the 1960s that governmental reform, burgeoning exports and rapid industrialization called the world's attention to a new Korea, proud, progressing and perseverant: a vigorous, optimistic people determined to shape their own destiny and build a better future, despite the sacrifices and hardships that the process might entail.

This transformed Korea might surprise those whose knowledge of the nation is drawn only from an examination of its 19th- and 20th-century trials. But students of its 5,000-year history will recognize the resiliency and fierce resolve of a durable people to maintain their national identity and independence.

This booklet, by briefly examining the history, culture, economy and other aspects of Korea, attempts to present a concise overview of Korea's time-honored legacy, modern achievements and the current direction of the Republic's nation-building.

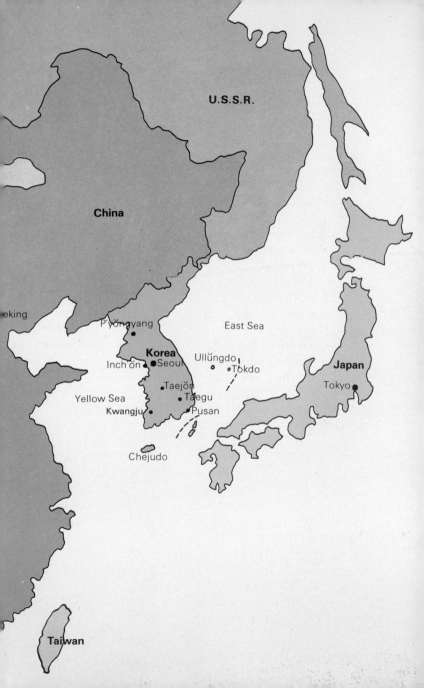

Land and People

Early morning fog blankets the valley of Namwon, Chŏllabuk-do Province.

The Land

The Korean peninsula is approximately 1,000km in north-south length, and 216km wide at its narrowest point and is separated from China's Shantung peninsula to the west by a 190km expanse of the Yellow Sea. The shortest distance between Korea and Japan is 206km.

To the east is the East Sea and to the south the Pacific Ocean. The Amnokkang (Yalu) and the Tumangang (Tumen) rivers separate the peninsula from Manchuria and Siberia to the north. The peninsula and all of its associated islands lie between 124°11'E and 131°53'E, and between 33°06'N and 43°01'N.

The peninsula area is 221,487km², or about 86,500 square miles. The land is presently divided into two parts—Communist North Korea and free South Korea (the Republic of Korea). The Republic of Korea's administrative control covers 99,117km² or about 45 percent of the total.

Korea is characterized by hills and mountains, which account for nearly 80 percent of its territory. Low hills are predominant in the south and west, and gradually yield to higher mountains in the east and north. Thus the western and southern slopes are gradual and meet with plains, low hills and winding river basins, while the eastern slopes plunge directly into the nearby East Sea.

The Nangnimsan range in the north and its southern extension, the T'aebaeksan range, form the peninsula divide and watershed along the east coast. While rarely exceeding 1,200m, the numerous peaks form a rugged, steep terrain. The roof of Korea, the Kaema Plateau, has an average elevation of 1,500m above sea level. Mt. Paektusan, located in the northwestern corner of the plateau, is the highest peak at 2,744m.

Many of Korea's highest summits occur along the Nangnimsan and T'aebaeksan ranges: Nangnimsan (2,014m), Kǔmgangsan (1,638m), Sǒraksan (1,708m) and T'aebaeksan (1,566m). These peaks form a spectacular collage of granitic pinnacles and deep, narrow canyons with many waterfalls and rapids. Lesser ranges and lateral spurs insure that one is seldom out of sight of mountains anywhere on the peninsula.

The peninsula as a whole is "tilted"—lifted in the east and somewhat sunken in the west and south, a process that began in the late Mesozoic Era. Thus the east coast is a nearly unbroken, precipitous shoreline of emergence, where the T'aebaeksan range rears up from the sea. Beaches are usually found where streams empty into the sea, often taking the form of coastal lagoons enclosed by sand spits and bars. The emergent shoreline and relatively short tidal range make these beaches and their facing waters particularly clean and popular. Ullǔngdo is the largest of the few islands off the east coast.

The west and south coasts are extremely irregular shorelines of submergence, as the rolling terrain follows the peninsular tilt into the East Sea and Pacific waters. Most of Korea's 3,400 islands are the result of these nearly hidden ridges and mountains, the most notable exception being the inactive volcanic island province of Cheju-do, some 140km off the southwest coast. The peninsular shoreline is estimated at 8,700km, and the islands add another 8,600km to that figure—the 17,300km total for a 1,000km peninsula indicates the severe indentation of the coastline.

The Pacific tidal currents force themselves into the Yellow Sea, thus forming a tidal range of six to 10 meters, and consequently broad mud flats along the west and southwest coasts, as well as such fine harbors as Inch'ǒn.

Most of the peninsula's myriad islands are found off the south and southwestern shores. The length of the southern coastline is nearly eight times its straight-line measurement. The mud flats common to the west coast are also found on the western third of the southern coast, while the eastern and central portions show submerged, almost fiord-like valleys and a much lessened tidal range, which results in both the fine harbors of Pusan and Mokp'o, as well as broad, clean beaches.

Most of Korea's rivers flow into the Yellow Sea and the Pacific waters to the south after draining the gentler western and southern slopes of the peninsula. The streams that do flow east from the T'aebaeksan Divide are short, straight and fast.

The gradual descent to the west and south has resulted in a relatively large number of streams for a territory the size of Korea. Six rivers exceed 400km in channel length: the Amnokkang (790km), the Tumangang (521km), the Han-gang (514km), the Kŭmgang (401km) and the Naktonggang (521km). In summer the rivers swell with the rainfall which accompanies the monsoon, often flooding valley plains once or twice a year. In the other seasons they are relatively dry.

In modern times the rivers have become increasingly important as sources of irrigation water. More than 70 percent of Korea's rice fields depend on river water irrigation, and large-scale, multipurpose dams provide flood control and produce electricity, as well as potable and industrial water supplies.

The people who settled in the fertile land of the Korean peninsula have developed a unique culture of their own. Overlooking Samnŭng Valley in Kyŏngju the large Buddhist image is an object of worship.

The nation's climate is temperate, influenced more by being an appendage to the world's largest continent than by the surrounding seas. It can generally be described as a humid, East Asian monsoonal climate. The hottest months are July and August; the coldest December and January.

Except in the extreme north, the bitterly cold Siberian-type weather often mistakenly associated with Korea does not occur. The milder winter of South Korea is commonly said to be characterized by three successive cold days, followed by four warmer days.

The rainy season falls sometime in June, July or August. During this period, an average of 50 percent of the total yearly precipitation is recorded.

Flora

Due to the Korean peninsula's long north-south stretch and topographic complexity, there are great variations in temperature and rainfall; the mean temperature throughout the four seasons ranges from 5° to 14°C, and rainfall from 500 to 1,500mm. Such a diversified environment makes the land a diversified floral region.

Many northern plants share common characteristics with those in Manchuria. Generally, alpine plants are found in the north and high mountain areas, while the central zones and the western lowlands are dominated by such temperate vegetation as broad-leaved deciduous trees. The southern coast and the offshore islands of Chejudo and Ullŭngdo host warm-temperate plants in abundance. Many of the evergreens growing in the

Neofinetie falcata Hu

Lotus

Hibiskus syriacus Linne

southern areas are identical or similar to those in the southwestern part of Japan.

While most of the flora in Korea has common elements with that found in neighboring regions, the peninsula's unique environment has given rise to a few endemic species.

The high annual average temperature (14°C) in the far south and offshore islands—Chejudo, Sohŭksando, and Ullŭngdo—fosters a great variety of plant species. More than 70 species of broad-leaved evergreens grace the shores of Chejudo. The southeast slope of Hallasan, the extinct volcano that created the island, boasts a greater abundance of warm-temperate vegetation than the northern side. The incidence of such species dwindles as the temperature contour line moves northward to the peninsula past Kŏmundo, Sohŭksando and other islands. Near Pusan and Mokp'o, both major southern ports, the number of broad-leaved evergreen species falls to less than 20.

Except for the high terrains of Hallasan and the T'aebaeksan range, the Korean peninsula has a typical temperate zone climate. Trees common in Korea are pine, maple, oak, larch, spruce, elm, willow, juniper, alder, birch, poplar, bamboo, acacia, paulownia and thuja. Fruit trees include apple, pear, peach, persimmon, orange, tangerine, fig, jujube, apricot, plum and Chinese quince trees in the far south. Common nut trees include walnut, chestnut, pine-nut and ginko.

July, the hottest month, is also the peak of the flowering season, although there are many species blossoming in spring and autumn. Woody plants tend to peak in May, and even in winter camellia bloom on the southern slopes and offshore islands. Flowering shrubs and plants such as azaleas, cherries, lilacs, forsythia, chrysanthemum, roses and countless wild flowers dot the landscape. The Rose of Sharon, the national flower, blooms from late spring to early autumn.

Fauna

Korea's geographical history, topography and climate divide the peninsula into highland and lowland districts. Included in the former are the Myohyangsan range, the Kaema Plateau and the more rugged terrain of the T'aebaeksan range. Most of the highland district lies about 1,000km from Mt. Paektusan along the Korean-Manchurian border, and is now covered with boreal forest. Many of the higher mountains supported glaciers during the Pleistocene period.

Animal life in the highland district is closely related to that in the boreal zones of Manchuria, mainland China, Siberia, Sakhalin and Hokkaido. Representative species are deer, roe deer, Amur goral, Manchurian weasel, brown bear, tiger, lynx, northern pika, water shrew, muskrat, Manchurian ring-necked pheasant, black grouse, hawk owl, pine grosbeak and the three-toed woodpecker.

The lowland peninsula area has a milder climate and includes the islands of Chejudo and Ullŭngdo. The fauna, closely related to that of southern Manchuria, central China and Japan, include black bear, river deer, Mandarin vole, white-bellied black (or Tristram's) woodpecker, fairy pitta and ring-necked pheasant.

Some 370 species of birds have been recorded in the South. Of these, 55 species are vagrants and one, Kuroda's Sheldrake, is probably extinct. The number of birds other than the vagrants and the extinct species is 314 species, of which 48 are permanent residents and

266 are migrants. Of the migratory birds, 112 species visit in the winter, 64 in the summer and 90 in the spring and autumn. One hundred and twelve species breed in Korea, including 48 indigenous species and 64 species of summer visitors.

There are 18 other species of birds recorded in North Korea: five are boreal residents of the high Paektusan terrain (black grouse, hawk owl, lesser-spotted woodpecker, three-toed woodpecker, willow tit), and the other 13 are vagrants.

There are six orders, 17 families, 48 genera and 78 species of indigenous mammals in Korea. These include 28 species of Chiroptera, 18 Rodentia, 16 Carnivora, 11 Insectivora, two Lagomorpha and seven Artiodactyla. There are 28 endemic sub-species on record as inhabiting the peninsula, but this is yet to be verified.

The large mammals are tiger, leopard, lynx, leopard cat, wolf, badger, bear, marten, weasel, wild boar, roe deer, deer and Amur goral. A few species such as bat, shrew, striped hamster, and muskrat are found only in North Korea. Also only in North Korea are tiger, lynx, two species of deer, Manchurian weasel and northern pika in the plateau regions of Paektusan.

Other wildlife species in the peninsula include 25 reptiles, 14 amphibians, and 130 freshwater fish.

Seventeen species of terrestrial mammals have been found on Chejudo Island. Wild boar, deer and wildcat are extinct and today the island is inhabited by roe deer, weasels, hamsters, field mice, house rats, and

A family portrait. Herons, such as these seen at Kangsŏng on the East Coast, have long been a favorite subject of Korean poems and paintings.

two bat species. There are also 207 forms of birds, and eight amphibians and reptilians of the island.

Ullŭngdo Island is devoid of endemic mammals. The known mammals of the island consist of six species (two of bat, one shrew, and three house rats that are commensals of man) all of which occur on the Korean mainland.

Twenty-three species of wildlife have been designated as national treasures, and 20 birds, two mammals and several insect species are designated endangered species. There are 17 localities designated as breeding grounds (eight egretries and heronries), passing or wintering grounds, and habitats for Tristram's woodpecker, fairy pitta, and loon. Also designated as national treasures are the domesticated silky fowl, Californian grey whale, the dog native to Chindo Island (called Chindogae), and four fish species.

Some 28 species of birds and eight species of mammals are designated for game purposes. Beginning in 1982, the government set the hunting season between November 1 and February 28 and will designate a different province each year as a legal hunting area.

The People

According to archaeological and linguistic studies, as well as legendary sources, tribes inhabiting the Altaic Mountains thousands of years ago started migrating eastward to Manchuria and Siberia. Some of them, believed to be Tungusic in origin, came as far east as the coasts of the Korean peninsula. They liked what they saw and settled there, soon to become a

24

homogeneous race sharing distinct physical characteristics, one language and one culture.

They are now known as the Korean people. Ethno-
logically, they are members of the Altaic family of
races, which includes the Turkish, Mongolian and
Tungusic peoples.

When the first migrants entered the Korean peninsula, estimated at around the third millennium B.C.,
they met natives called Paleoasians. Archaeologists
have uncovered two types of pottery in Korea
which they feel come from the people of two different
ages: comb-patterned pottery of a Neolithic Age people and plain pottery of a Bronze Age people.

The patterned pottery, believed to be the product of
a food-gathering, hunting and fishing people, has
been discovered near river banks and along the sea-
shore while the plain pottery, believed to come from a
food-producing people, has been unearthed mostly in
the hilly regions of the country. Most of the natives
were subsequently driven north, to Sakhalin, Kam-
chatka, and to the Arctic region, while a few were
assimilated into the new settlers. It must be noted here
that some of the migrants from the Altaic Mountains
kept on the move, eventually reaching the southwestern shores of Japan.

In this manner, there has been a racial flow from
Korea to Japan since ancient times. There is much
historic evidence testifying to the fact that the Koreans
have contributed appreciably to the Japanese racial
stock formation, as well as to cultural development.

In the latter half of the seventh century the Koreans
were placed, for the first time in their long history,
under one rule, that of Unified Shilla. This political
unity was to consolidate the homogeneity of the
Koreans, unifying them with one language and culture.
Strong racial consciousness and sense of unity has

Young couples and students enjoy a performance at an open-air

stage in the heart of Seoul's shopping district.

Population by Age Group (1980)

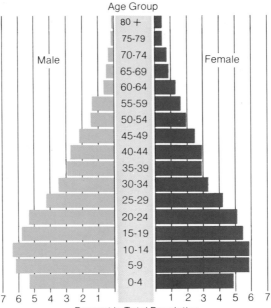

Age Group

	Male		Female	
80 +				
75-79				
70-74				
65-69				
60-64				
55-59				
50-54				
45-49				
40-44				
35-39				
30-34				
25-29				
20-24				
15-19				
10-14				
5-9				
0-4				

7 6 5 4 3 2 1   1 2 3 4 5 6 7

Percent in Total Population

thus become an inalienable Korean quality, which no amount of invasion and repression—from the Mongol hordes to the Japanese colonialists—could ever erase.

Only recently have outside influences, urbanization and rapid economic development wrought great changes in the social structure and philosophic outlook of the Korean people. However, a renewed confidence and pride have resulted in an evaluation of the new in the light of traditional values—especially those of filial piety and patriotism. Confucianism, Buddhism, Shamanism and other indigenous beliefs and systems unite with Christianity and Western schools of thought to provide Koreans with a unique perspective on themselves and the world.

Historical experience and the rigors of modern life have made Koreans highly competitive and disciplined. Annual reports by such organizations as the International Labor Organization consistently declare them to be at or near the top of national productivity ratings. Nevertheless, they are a generous, warmhearted people with an earthy sense of humor and a love of music and dance.

Traditionally, Korea was divided into four rigid classes—the *yangban* or upper class, the middle class, commoners and outcasts. Social relations were governed from the time of the Yi Dynasty of the Chosŏn Kingdom (1392-1910) by the Confucian system of ethics, which emphasized hierarchical social relationships, filial piety and patriotism. The extended family was the basis of social and economic life. A classical, Confucian education was necessary for advancement in government and was reserved for the *yangban* class.

Japanese colonialism, the division of the country, war, the industrial revolution and the accompanying Western values have all combined to transform the traditional social system. While social class is still based on education, occupation and wealth, these are no longer hereditary nor restricted to the old *yangban* class.

There is an increasingly large middle class of professionals, mid-level industrial managers, small businessmen and skilled workers, with relatively small upper and lower classes. Social mobility is great, especially among those capable of taking part in the economic successes of the industrial revolution.

Family ties are still strong, and filial piety and patriotism are resurgent values. Still, the nuclear family has largely supplanted the extended, three-generation home, especially in cities. Large numbers of well-educated women are assuming a much more active social role.

The population of the Republic of Korea in 1985 was about 41,209,000. The rate of population growth has been declining in recent years from a high in 1961 of 2.9 percent to a low in 1985 of 1.53 percent, due to a successful family planning program, increased urbanization, a higher standard of living and a trend toward later marriages. The population of Korea is very young with 55.7 percent under 25 years of age.

The population of the country is becoming increasingly urban, with the farm population in 1984 accounting for 22.2 percent of the total. This urbanization is characterized by the dominance of Seoul over the life of the nation. Nearly 20 percent of the population lives in the capital city, which is the center of government, industry, education and culture. Impressive gains in rural development and the designation of industrial estates outside of the capital area, however, have helped to balance the attractiveness of Seoul, as will a number of satellite cities being built on its outskirts.

Language

The Korean alphabet, *han-gŭl*, is a phonetic system consisting of 10 vowels and 14 consonants which are combined to form syllables. Syllables consist of a minimum of two and a maximum of four letters. Unlike Chinese characters, there is no symbolism involved in *han-gŭl*, which is one of the most scientific writing systems in the world.

Before the creation of *han-gŭl*, written communication was by way of Chinese characters which were very difficult to learn and thus were the monopoly of a learned upper class which was also the ruling class. In 1443, King Sejong the Great (r. 1418-1450), the fourth king of the Chosŏn Kingdom (1392-1910), commissioned a group of scholars to develop *hun-minchŏngŭm*, or "script for the people," which would make reading and writing of the Korean language an easy matter for all people, regardless of class. This project was greatly opposed by many officials of the court and learned Confucian scholars because they feared that it would degrade literature and bring it down to the "level of dust."

The king, however, persisted and the result is, undoubtedly, the greatest cultural legacy of the Korean people. *Han-gŭl* has enabled Korea to have one of the highest literacy rates in the world, and *han-gŭl* typewriters and the ease of printing in *han-gŭl* have contributed to the speedy flow of information.

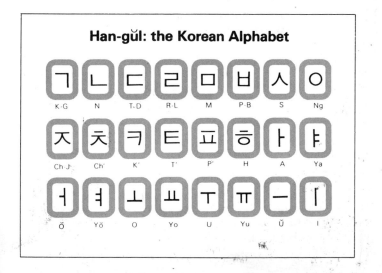

Han-gŭl: the Korean Alphabet

ㄱ	ㄴ	ㄷ	ㄹ	ㅁ	ㅂ	ㅅ	ㅇ
K·G	N	T·D	R·L	M	P·B	S	Ng

ㅈ	ㅊ	ㅋ	ㅌ	ㅍ	ㅎ	ㅏ	ㅑ
Ch·J	Ch'	K'	T'	P'	H	A	Ya

ㅓ	ㅕ	ㅗ	ㅛ	ㅜ	ㅠ	ㅡ	ㅣ
Ŏ	Yŏ	O	Yo	U	Yu	Ŭ	I

A Combware pot, Neolithic Age, circa 3,000 B.C.

Beginning of History

Toward the end of the Neolithic Age, the people on the Korean peninsula began to be divided into clans. Families became family groups, which in turn formed clans. Frequent and peaceful contacts between clans resulting from exogamy led to a gradual softening of the fierce exclusiveness and animosity. Gradually larger regional groups began to emerge, each consisting of several clans.

The distribution of dolmens and other relics indicate that tribes with ruling classes and later larger political units first emerged in the north. The first of these was Ancient Chosŏn. This tribal league dominated the territory between the Liao River in southern Manchuria and the Taedonggang River in central North Korea.

The league's dominant clan, which hence produced most of the rulers, was a bear-totem family whose legendary founder was Tan-gun, the mythical progenitor of the Korean people. The legend goes that a heavenly king, Hwanin, sent his son, Hwanung, to earth where he married a bear-turned-woman and they gave birth to Tan-gun 24 centuries before the birth of Christ. Tan-gun welded together various primitive tribes into a single kingdom.

The Tan-gun era, called Ancient Chosŏn, lasted 1,200 years followed by the Kija era of about 99 years. Later, Ancient Chosŏn was split into various communities. Three tribal states of Mahan, Chinhan and Pyŏnhan were established in southern Korea. The

Sottae *like this were erected at villages as symbolic of a prayer for a good harvest and in the belief that they would protect against fire, wind, rain, disease and evil spirits.*

"Three Hans," as they were called, gained a considerable reputation for tribal organization, unique customs and handicraft. The remnants of Ancient Chosŏn, in northern Korea, gave way to the Han Empire of China in 109 B.C. Han China established four colonies—Lolang, Chenfan, Hsuantu and Lintun.

The Three Kingdoms

Records indicate that the Chinese soon lost their influence in the three colonies other than Lolang, and in their place rose various tribal leagues. Puyŏ was founded on the Sungari River in Manchuria; Koguryŏ on the Tongga River, a tributary of the Yalu; Okchŏ on the plains along the northeast coast of the Korean peninsula; and Tong-ye, south of Okchŏ.

Among these tribal leagues, Koguryŏ was the first to mature into a kingdom. It conquered the neighboring tribes one after another, annexing Okchŏ and Tong-ye in the east, absorbing Puyŏ in the north and driving the Chinese out of Lolang.

Koguryŏ (37 B.C.-A.D. 668) was firmly established as a state power by the first century A.D. They clashed frequently with the Chinese while Paekche (18 B.C.-A.D. 660) amassed power in the south, and the two Korean states finally came into conflict in the late fourth century. The following centuries witnessed the growth of Shilla's (57 B.C.-A.D. 935) more fully organized state power.

Koguryŏ was the first to adopt Buddhism as royal creed in 372, followed by Paekche in 384 and Shilla in 528. Buddhist scriptures were brought from China along with Confucian statecraft. Koguryŏ compiled

100 volumes of state history before the introduction of Buddhism; Paekche compiled a history prior to 384; and only Shilla began compiling its history after the introduction of Buddhism.

Koguryŏ, Paekche and Shilla developed state organizations, using Confucian and Buddhist hierarchical structures with the king at the pinnacle. State codes were promulgated, and the three states competed in strengthening Buddhist-Confucian state power to attempt territorial expansion.

At this juncture Shilla developed the *Hwarang*, a voluntary youth organization. This "flower of youth corps" was trained in the arts of war, literary taste and community life, partly via pilgrimages. This movement of Buddhist-Confucian virtues became popular and contributed to the strength of Shilla.

While Shilla built up amicable relations with Tang China, Koguryŏ fought fiercely with both Sui and Tang China. A Koguryŏ ambush destroyed a massive invading Sui army in 612, contributing to the fall of Sui that shortly followed. Tang rose and invaded Koguryŏ in 644, 648 and 655, but walls and fortifications along the Liao River frustrated all attempts.

Shilla persuaded Tang China to assist in the conquest of Paekche and then Koguryŏ. Shilla, the last of the three to achieve statehood, finally defeated the other two, but was unable to dominate Koguryŏ's Manchurian territories. Tang's intentions became clear when Tang generals were appointed to administer former Paekche and Koguryŏ territories in 660 and 668, respectively.

Kim Yu-shin, Shilla's foremost general, led operations against the Chinese in 671, capturing the Chinese administrative headquarters in Paekche the same year. The Chinese army pressed its claim to Paekche and Koguryŏ territories until 735, when they recog-

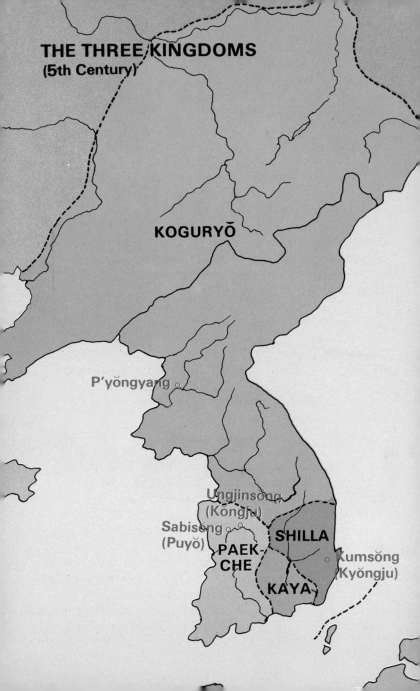

THE THREE KINGDOMS
(5th Century)

KOGURYŌ

P'yŏngyang

Ungjinsŏng
(Kongju)

Sabisŏng
(Puyŏ)

SHILLA

PAEK
CHE

Kumsŏng
(Kyŏngju)

KAYA

These four maps show the changing political configuration of the Korean peninsula from the time of the Three Kingdoms through the Chosŏn Kingdom period. The Shilla Kingdom first unified the territory south of the Taedonggang River in 668 and the peninsula was not again divided until after World War II.

THE KORYŌ KINGDOM
(11th Century)

KORYŌ

○ Kaegyŏng
(Kaesŏng)

THE UNIFIED SHILLA AND PARHAE KINGDOMS
(8th Century)

PARHAE

○ Sanggyŏng

SHILLA

○ Kŭmsŏng
(Kyŏngju)

THE CHOSŎN KINGDOM
(15th Century)

CHOSŎN

○ Hansŏng
(Seoul)

CHRONOLOGICAL TABLE

	KOREA	JAPAN	CHINA
B.C.	Palaeolithic Age Neolithic Age		
			Shang Dynasty (1600—) Chou (1027-1256) Spring and Autumn Era (770-476)
700	Bronze Age Ancient Chosŏn		Warring States Era (475-221)
300	Early Iron Age Puyŏ	Yayoi Period	Ch'in Dynasty (221-206) Western Han Dynasty (206 B.C.-A.D.9)
200			
100	Samhan (Three Han States)		
	Three Kingdoms Period Shilla (57 B.C.—A.D. 935) Koguryŏ (37 B.C.—A.D. 668) Paekche (18 B.C.—A.D. 660)		
A.D.	Kaya (42—562)		Hsin Dynasty (8—25) Eastern Han Dynasty (26—221)
100		Tumulus Period	Period of Division (220-581) Three Kingdoms Period (220—280)
300			Six Dynasties (439—589)
500		Asuka Period (552—645)	Sui Dynasty (581—618)
600	Parhae (669—928) Unified Shilla Kingdom (618—935)	Hakuho Period (645—710)	T'ang Dynasty (618—907)
700		Nara Period (710—794) Heian Period (794—1185)	
800 900	Koryŏ Kingdom (918—1392)		Ten Kingdoms, Five Dynasties Period (907—979) Northern Sung Dynasty (960—1279)
1000 1100		Kamakura Period (1185—1392)	Southern Sung Dynasty (1127—1279)
1200			Yuan Dynasty (1206—1358)
1300	Chosŏn Kingdom (1392—1910)	Ashikaga Period (1392—1572)	Ming Dynasty (1368—1662)
1400 1500		Momoyama Period (1576-1600)	
1600		Tokugawa Period (1603-1867)	Ch'ing Dynasty (1616—1912)
1700 1800	Taehan Empire Proclaimed (1897)	The Meiji Restoration (1867-)	
1900	Annexation by Japan (1910) Establishment of the Republic of Korea (1945)		Establishment of the Republic of China (1911)

nized Shilla's right to all territory south of the Tae-donggang River. Shilla thus became the first state to encompass the Korean peninsula and the people of the three kingdoms.

A former Koguryŏ general formed an army of Koguryŏ and Malgal (a Tungusic tribe) people and led a migration to Chinese-held territory. There they founded the state of Chin, renamed Parhae in 713. Ruled by mostly Koguryŏ people, Parhae came to control most former Koguryŏ territories.

Parhae territory and prosperity peaked in the first half of the ninth century. Parhae extended from the Sungari and Amur rivers in northern Manchuria to the northern provinces of modern Korea. When the Tang Dynasty fell and the Khitan conquered Parhae in 926 on their way to domination over much of Manchuria and northern China, the predominantly Korean Parhae ruling class came south to join the newly founded Koryŏ Kingdom which replaced Shilla. While the Manchurian portion of Parhae was lost, the area south of the Amnokkang-Tuman-gang boundary was restored.

Unified Shilla (668-935)

Shilla power and prosperity peaked in the middle of the eighth century. During this period came attempts to establish an ideal Buddhist state. Consequently Sŏkkuram (a stone cave shrine) and Pulguksa Temple (the Buddhist state temple) were built. Woodblock printing of Buddhist scriptures began, too. The oldest imprint of the Dahrani sutra, printed circa 706-751, came to light during the recent restoration of a three-story pagoda at Pulguksa Temple.

The cultural spirit of Shilla. From a 5th-century gold crown to a stoneware vessel of a noble warrior on horseback, Shilla artifacts reveal the

sophistication and humor of Shilla artisans. Every age and aspect of Korean society seem to have been touched in some way by the variety and beauty of artistic expression.

The Shilla people enjoyed an affluent life. The capital city of Kyŏngju prospered, linked by 10 kilometers of sheltered corridors. Wŏnhyo, a prominent monk, founded a new Buddhist sect among the common people, making it a popular religion rather than only a royal creed.

In the peaceful remainder of the eighth century the desire for learning grew. Mid-upper class scholars invented the *Idu* system for transcribing Korean words, and the growing need for scholarly work led to a quasi-civil service examination in 788.

Buddhism began to deteriorate as the nobility enjoyed a luxurious life. The new *Sŏn* Buddhist sect rose in the remote mountain areas as conflict among the nobility in outlying districts intensified. The throne continually lost power as *Chingol* (royal-aristocratic) clan conflicts grew.

Thus ninth-century Shilla was shaken by intra-clan conflicts around the throne and disturbances in district administration. Many local leaders rebelled against the Shilla throne. The government prohibited new temples and extravagant decoration in 806, further alienating scholars and other talented Shilla people.

Koryŏ (918-1392)

A turbulent era began with Shilla being torn into pieces by rebel leaders in 900. Latter Paekche was proclaimed in Chŏnju and Kung-ye proclaimed Latter Koguryŏ the following year at Kaesŏng. Wang Kŏn, the last rebel leader, was Kung-ye's first minister. In

This early 7th century, gilt bronze image of Maitreya, the Buddha of the Future, is one of Korea's most beautiful Buddhist works.

918 he gained the support of landlords and merchants whose economic and political power overwhelmed the Shilla government and then enabled Wang Kŏn to overthrow Kung-ye for misdemeanors and malpractices. He was enthroned as the founder king of Koryŏ and was given the posthumous title of T'aejo (r. 918-943).

He easily raided Latter Paekche in 934, and received their surrender in 935. The following year he accepted the abdication of Shilla King Kyŏngsunwang (r. 927-935).

T'aejo at first left the provincial magnates undisturbed and carefully placated the Shilla aristocracy, giving former King Kyŏngsunwang the highest post in his government. He legitimated his rule somewhat by marrying into the Shilla royal clan. His lenient policy and marriage ties kept the rebellious local lords in line.

King Kwangjong (r. 949-975) emancipated slaves in 956, restoring to commoner status those unjustly bonded, thus increasing state revenue. Two years later he installed a civil service examination system to recruit officials by merit. King Kyŏngjong (r. 975-981), the fifth Koryŏ monarch, began the practice of allotting land and forest lots to officials. King Sŏngjong (r. 981-997) in 982, as recommended by Confucian scholar Ch'oe Sŭng-no, paved the way to Confucian rule. District officials were appointed by the central government and all privately-owned arms were recast into agricultural tools.

The government was modeled after the Tang system, with the addition of officials empowered to admonish the throne and censor royal decisions. Such internal order enabled Koryŏ to withstand the foreign invasions.

In the north, Jurchen Mongol tribes grew stronger

in the Korean border area of Manchuria. War-weary Koryŏ King Hyŏnjong (r.1009-1031) ordered the carving of the *Tripitaka,* imploring Buddha's aid. The completed first carving of wood blocks comprised some 6,000 chapters of Buddhist scriptures.

Then in 1126, all Koryŏ palace buildings, including tens of thousands of books in the royal library and national academy, were destroyed in a fire set by the father-in-law of King Injong (r. 1122-1146). There was no way to get replacements from Sung China, and books printed from wood blocks were prohibitively expensive. Then came the idea of typography, and Koryŏ cast the world's first known movable metal type with bronze coin-casting technology. Many titles were printed in limited editions from metal type around the mid-12th century.

The *Samguksagi* (History of the Three Kingdoms) was compiled by the Confucian scholar Kim Pu-shik in 1145 at the order of King Injong. A monk named Iryŏn compiled the *Samgukyusa* (Memorabilia of the Three Kingdoms), an important source of history and traditions not found in the *Samguksagi.*

Despite these advances, there were conflicts between literati officials and the warrior class, as the latter had been generally degraded and was paid less. In 1170 the warrior class rose up against the literati and settled the score with bloodshed. Mongol power was consolidated about this time, and with the new Sung iron technology the Mongols conquered Chin in 1215. After this, Koryŏ was plagued by consecutive Mongol invasions and the Koryŏ court fled to Kanghwado Island in 1232.

A Mongol invasion swept over Koryŏ in 1238, destroying the splendid Shilla pagoda of Hwangnyongsa Temple. The second *Tripitaka Koreana* was carved by the court on Kanghwado, this time consisting of

80,000 wood blocks engraved on both sides, and again dedicated to obtaining Buddha's protection against the Mongols. The Koryŏ people had reached a consensus to resist the foreign invaders.

By 1368 the Ming Dynasty had begun its 300-year rule, and by 1382 the new dynasty controlled all of China proper. Freed from Mongol domination, Koryŏ began reforming its government. King Kongminwang (r. 1351-1374) came to the throne in 1351 and removed pro-Mongol aristocrats and military officers, who then plotted and botched a coup.

A second major internal problem was the land-grant system. Kongminwang's attempt at land reform met with insurmountable opposition from the officials who were to implement the reforms, as they were the owners of the affected land.

A third problem was growing animosity between Buddhists and Confucian scholars. Normally Buddhism and Confucian creeds coexisted with little conflict; however, many Korean scholars were imbued with the neo-Confucian doctrine advocated by Chu Hsi in the late 12th century, just before the advent of the Mongols. The new Confucian scholars rejected the Buddhist concept of denouncing one's family ties to become a monk, as strong family and social relationships were the very basis of Confucian philosophy. They criticized the wealth and power of the monasteries, as well as the great expense incurred by the state for Buddhist festivals.

In addition to these internal problems, Japanese pirates had changed from hit-and-run bandits into organized military marauders, penetrating deep into the country. A general, Yi Sŏng-gye, distinguished himself by repelling the pirates in a series of successful engagements: his next opponents were to be the declining Koryŏ monarchy and nobility.

A mid-12th century Koryŏ Kingdom celadon.

往厤牙説敢違總土東海
黃公
今跋尾撟打者誰識八中
顆同
甲午南立日

An 18th-century tiger painting.

Chosŏn (1392-1910)

Neo-Confucian ideology became political capital in General Yi Sŏng-gye's fight against the declining Koryŏ monarchy and nobility. In a careful attempt to give the new dynasty every appearance of legitimacy instead of ascending the throne by right of conquest, Yi Sŏng-gye had Koryŏ's Supreme Council, now filled with his own supporters, declare in 1392 that the Koryŏ Kingdom had come to an end and that he was the rightful king. He was given the posthumous title T'aejo.

The new kingdom was named Chosŏn, though it is known in the West by the dynastic name of Yi. The construction of a Confucian state was given top priority.

To promote Confucian learning, movable metal type was cast for Confucian classics and historical literature in 1403. The repeated casting of new fonts brought improvements in typography.

Sejong's Confucian Humanism

King Sejong the Great (r. 1418-1450), the fourth sovereign of the dynasty, was the greatest Chosŏn monarch, and his enlightened Confucian rule set a standard against which all subsequent rulers were measured.

He was noted for his mastery of Confucian learning and his ability to cope with *yangban* (the upper class composed of the literati from whom military and civil officials were chosen) scholars. His mid-15th century rule was marked by progressive ideas in administration, linguistics, science, music, medical science and humanistic studies. He established the Hall of Talented Scholars to promote research in institutional traditions and politico-economics, and many young scholars received government support. His efforts to improve movable metal type brought a revolution in printing.

Sejong showed great concern for the peasants by providing drought and flood relief. At his order, Chŏng Ch'o compiled the *Straight Talk on Farming*, based on interviews with experienced elder peasants. Sejong ordered the development and nationwide distribution of the pluviometer in 1442, preceding Gastelli's pluviometer by almost two hundred years.

Perhaps his most celebrated achievement was the creation of the Korean alphabet, *han-gŭl*, to provide a script for the vernacular language. Until that time, the Chinese ideograms were adopted for literary purposes in Korea, which meant not only learning a grammatical system radically different from Korean, but also the laborious memorization of thousands of Chinese characters. King Sejong conceived the idea of devising a system of writing the Korean language phonetically, so that all his people would be able to learn to read and write easily.

The king assigned a committee of scholars to work on the creation of symbols which would represent the sounds of the Korean language. The result was the invention of a system of 17 consonants and 11 vowels, which King Sejong promulgated in 1446. The *han-gŭl* alphabet possesses geometric beauty, simplicity and phonetic accuracy, and can be learned in a matter of hours.

Sejong's concern for his people showed itself again in the compilation of a 265-chapter compendium on Chinese medicine, as well as the *Compendium on Indigenous Medicine*, which was completed in 1433 with 85 chapters and thousands of entries. Another book on collecting medicinal materials was published in *han-gŭl*.

Astronomical science apparently fascinated Sejong: a sun dial, water clock, solar system orrery, celestial globes, astronomical maps and almanacs of the seven known planets were made at his promoting. He caused notation for Korean and Chinese music to be devised or revised, and musical instruments improved.

Sejong's land tax reform, health policies and invention of the Korean alphabet improved the people's lives and engendered a modern national consciousness. His economic, scientific and scholarly achievements deserve global recognition.

Japanese Invasion

In the late 1500s, a warlord named Hideyoshi Toyotomi rose to power in Japan. Having succeeded in imposing his rule on the whole country, Hideyoshi was in search of new worlds to conquer. He sent envoys to Korea to reopen relations, which were suspended due to incessant incursions by Japanese pirates. Hideyoshi's message also contained a demand that Korea give free passage to the Japanese army in their invasion of China. Korea, committed to good relations with Ming China, rejected the Japanese demand, and Hideyoshi invaded Korea with 150,000 troops in the spring of 1592.

Korean defenders heroically resisted the aggressors. But the heavily outnumbered and unprepared forces were no match for the Japanese troops equipped with muskets, a weapon totally new to the Koreans. Seoul fell within two weeks of the beginning of the invasion.

King Sŏnjo (r. 1567-1608) and the royal princes fled to the northern provinces and appealed to Ming

China for aid. Meanwhile, as the Japanese generals squabbled among themselves, Admiral Yi Sun-shin conducted a brilliant series of operations in the Korean Strait, destroying numerous Japanese ships. The ironclad "turtle boats" Admiral Yi perfected and utilized were more than a match for anything then afloat.

The triumphant Japanese were soon fighting a combined Ming Chinese-Korean army. Cut off from supplies and reinforcements by Admiral Yi, the Japanese generals began to lose confidence. A Korean volunteer army in the southern provinces harassed them with guerrilla tactics, while disease and malnutrition took further tolls. Peace negotiations began between the Ming general and the Japanese, who had lost the will to fight and had begun to retreat, stalked by volunteer peasant forces and contingents of Buddhist monks.

Negotiations dragged on for five years until Hideyoshi again sent his army in 1597. This invasion encompassed only Kyŏngsang-do and part of the Chŏlla-do provinces. They soon retreated before the volunteers, and then began evacuating upon the death of Hideyoshi. Admiral Yi was killed in his attempt to smash the Japanese retreat during a climactic naval battle. The war ended at last, with grave impact upon Korea, Ming China and Japan.

Both the Korean land and people were devastated by the Hideyoshi Invasions. Many artisans and technicians were taken by the retreating Japanese, and arable land was only one-third of the prewar acreage.

Japan, on the other hand, achieved a peaceful, centralized feudal society under Hideyoshi's successor, Ieyasu Tokugawa. The importation of neo-Confucianism and the study of Korean medicinal materials and therapy helped Japanese scholars make significant contributions to their society. Movable metal type expedited book printing and Korean artisans captured by the Japanese army developed ceramic and textile products.

After the Tokugawa takeover, Japan sought peaceful relations with Korea in the hope of gaining even greater cultural benefits. For Ming China, the results of the Hideyoshi Invasions were catastrophic. The economic setback suffered in the campaign led to the collapse of the dynasty.

Postwar Readjustment

Reorganizing defense forces and increasing state revenues were the urgent postwar tasks. The Office of Border Defense was elevated to *de facto* decision-making status and a national defense council was formed with state councilors, ministers and military staff.

Arts of war proven effective against Japanese pirates on the south China coast were given first priority, but this training required an additional tax from the peasants. Privately-owned bondsmen, previously exempted from military service, were recruited for training, giving them a new reason to consider themselves equal to commoners.

Reconstructing palace buildings and printing lost books, ledgers and records further strained the state budget. Wooden printing type was carved at the Army Training Center due to a metal shortage incurred by arms production. Books were sold to pay expenses, contrary to prewar practice.

Medical aid for the disease-stricken populace was also urgently needed. The compilation of a *Treasury of Korean Medicine*, started during the war, was completed in 1610. The stronger position of awakened peasants during and after the war was reflected in this state response.

Kwanghaegun (r. 1608-1623) tried to restore the Confucian state, and sent an army of 10,000 to help Ming China resist the Manchus—but the Manchus were victorious and Kwanghaegun was deposed by a newly ascendant group.

Like the Mongols before them, the Manchus did not want a hostile Korea on their flank when they drove into China. In 1627, taking advantage of a dynastic dispute, they crossed the Yalu River and soon overran much of the country. Yet to recover from the devastation wrought by the Hideyoshi Invasions, Korea was in no condition to mount an effective resistance. The court fled to Kanghwado Island.

Wishing to conserve their forces for a major attack on China, the Manchus were content at this point simply to ensure that Korea would be unable to act against them.

The peace treaty concluded after the first Manchu invasion stipulated that Korea would aid the Manchus rather than the Ming. When the Chosŏn ruler refused to accept a suzerain-vassal status in 1636, the Manchu ruler—enthroned as the Ching Emperor of China—invaded Korea again. King Injo fled, but later capitulated on the bank of the Han River, agreeing to break relations with the defeated Ming and to send princes as hostages.

Korea-Centered Studies

Pragmatic studies, begun in the early 17th century, continued to grow, as many scholars sought solutions to social problems through administrative reforms in land distribution and agricultural improvements: the emphasis was on limiting land-holdings and applying egalitarian principles to land tenure.

Yi Ik proposed a society opened by abolishing class distinctions and emancipating bondsmen. Pak Chiwon's stories ridiculed the idle, unproductive and pretentious *yangban* way of life, and advocated an improvement in agricultural equipment, irrigation systems and new cultivation techniques. Other scholars recommended that Korea introduce Western techniques and participate in international trade along with Ching China. They were the vanguard of a movement destined to destroy the traditional *yangban* disdain for technology and commerce.

Concern for Korea's identity revived even in the midst of absorbing Western culture and techniques from China. Koreans studied their own history, geography, language and epigraphy with renewed vigor. Painters turned from traditional China-oriented styles and began to portray the life and scenery of Korea.

This cultural independence surfaced in historiography as well. An Chŏng-bok's *The Main Currents of Korean History* emphasized the roles of those who expelled foreign invaders, and reprimanded the ruling class for concentrating on how best to exploit the people. Geography kept pace by developing woodblock cartography, and Chŏng Sang-gi's ingenious scaling device stimulated Korean mapping. Kim Chŏng-ho created a scale map of great precision based on his indefatigable travels throughout the peninsula.

The compilation of books accelerated in the 18th century. King Chŏngjo (r. 1776-1800) employed young scholars of mixed origin in his newly-established Inner Royal Library for such projects as the *Encyclopedia of the Eastern Country,* the *Collated Grand State Codes* and the *Compendium of Korean Music.*

Korean typographical enterprise stimulated developments in China. The famed Chinese encyclopedia *Kuchin Tushu Chicheng* was printed for the first time with movable metal type in 1782.

Emergence of Modern Culture

Yi Su-gwang (1563-1628), probably the earliest thinker to come into contact with Catholic and European culture, stressed that knowledge was of no value without action, just as enforcement is essential to the substance of law. His *Classified Dictionary of the Grassy Peak*, published in 1614, was similar in inspiration to the work of French encyclopedists. It greatly expanded the knowledge available to Koreans of European and Southeast Asian countries, and explained the nature of Catholicism for the first time.

Equality, human dignity, equal opportunity, public welfare and the advancement of the national economy were the conspicuous philosophic principles that emerged in this period. This development in 17th- and 18th-century Korea is in some respects reminiscent of the Western European Renaissance.

Economic developments and social improvements burgeoned in the early 18th century. People thought foreign ideas in general and European commercial enterprise in particular should be seriously considered. Some literati-officials advocated a thorough reform of national finance, and the central government examined the proposal. Its implementation, however, was thwarted by a struggle for power.

The government persecuted Catholics severely in 1801 and 1839, dispersing the converts to outlying districts, where Catholicism spread among impoverished farmers and *yangban*. At the Korean court in this final stage of the dynasty, King Ch'ŏlchong (r. 1849-

1863) died in 1864, leaving no male heir. A dowager queen named a new king and the choice fell upon the second son of a royal descendant named Yi Ha-ŭng. The boy ascended the throne and Yi Ha-ŭng was made regent and given the title Taewon-gun.

Taewon-gun turned out to be one of the most powerful personalities in the history of the Chosŏn Kingdom. Within a short time after his son's accession he was in complete control of the court and government, and no clan or faction could dare stand against him. He effected a series of sweeping financial and administrative reforms to strengthen the royal authority. He vigorously opposed the accelerating infiltration of foreign commercial interests. In the spring of 1866, the government again decreed a persecution of Catholics. Aroused by this measure, a French fleet appeared near Inch'ŏn and hostilities broke out on Kanghwado Island.

Alien Encroachment and Reactions

During the late 19th century insistent demands were made for commercial relations by the English, the Russians and other Europeans. A Prussian merchant E. Oppert was refused trade with Korea twice in 1866, and in that same year the American ship *General Sherman* sortied into Korean waters to force the Korean government to open commercial relations. The ship reached P'yŏngyang on the Taedonggang River with a cargo of European merchandise, but infuriated the Koreans by using excessive force in dealing with Korean soldiers and civilians. The *General Sherman* was attacked and set afire.

From 1868 Japan began pressing Korea to open negotiations aimed at revising their traditional relations. The *General Sherman* incident intensified U.S.

efforts to force Korea to open her ports, and in 1871, five years after the French were repelled there, Washington commissioned its Asian fleet to invade Kanghwado Island. The American troops were also repulsed and their fleet retreated from Korean waters.

Japan had been anxiously following developments in Korea, looking for an opportunity to open the country. When Taewon-gun was forced to relinquish his regency in 1873 by Queen Min and her faction, renewed Japanese attempts were made to open relations. After an envoy carrying the Japanese emperor's formal proposal returned home empty-handed, Japan sent two battleships to Pusan and Inch'ŏn where skirmishes with Korean defenders occurred. Judging that Korea had been sufficiently impressed, Japan dispatched a delegation to Kanghwado Island accompanied by six naval ships in January 1876. Faced with the demonstration of force, the Korean government very reluctantly sent negotiators to Kanghwado, where a treaty of amity was drawn up. An addendum to this treaty, consisting of a trade accord and a customs agreement, all drafted by Japan, was signed in July 1876. These instruments provided a legal basis for Japanese aggression by granting such privileges as extraterritoriality, exemption from customs duties, and legal recognition of Japanese currency in the ports to be opened to foreign trade.

The Korea-U.S. Treaty of Commerce was concluded and signed on May 22, 1882. Great Britain and Germany quickly negotiated similar treaties which their home governments refused to ratify until they had been revised to lower the tariff rates. Revised treaties were signed on November 26, 1883. A treaty of commerce was signed with Russia on June 25, 1884, and was followed on August 8, 1888 by another agreement governing Korean-Russian overland commerce.

Also signed during this period was a treaty of commerce with France, and an agreement with Japan concerning the commercial activites of Japanese residents in Korea.

The Tonghak Struggle of 1894

Tonghak (Eastern Learning) was based on the doctrine of the equality of all people and the unity of God with man. Despite the religious aspect, *Tonghak's* main concern was a call for realistic national stability and security. Alarmed by *Tonghak's* growing popularity, the Korean government executed its founder, Ch'oe Che-u, in 1864 on charges of sedition.

His movement lived on, however, and poverty-stricken farmers flocked to the *Tonghak* standard. Large-scale demonstrations broke out in 1892 in the Chŏlla-do and Ch'ungch'ŏng-do provinces; in 1893, the *Tonghak* believers went to Seoul and staged a demonstration before the royal palace, but were dispersed by the army. About 20,000 *Tonghak* followers assembled at Poŭn, Ch'ungch'ŏngbuk-do Province, and proclaimed their determination to reject Japan and the West. In 1894, Chŏn Pong-jun assumed leadership of the *Tonghak* in the Chŏlla-do provinces, where cruel exploitation of already hard-pressed farmers continued after the construction of a new reservoir.

Their peaceful protests having proved fruitless, the farmers resorted to violence. The government countered with draconian measures, as an inspector from Seoul ordered wholesale executions. Chŏn then led a larger uprising and defeated the government army occupying the provincial capital at Chŏnju.

After considerable success in the southern provinces, the *Tonghak* leaders acceded to conciliatory promises by the government and ceased hostilities.

King Kojong (r. 1863-1907), nevertheless, had appealed to China for help in putting down the rebels, and the Japanese had also seized the opportunity to send forces to Korea.

On July 25, 1894, the Japanese attacked Chinese warships near Asan Bay along the west coast and also Chinese foot units in the Seoul area, touching off what was described later as the Sino-Japanese War. The Chinese lost nearly all the battles.

The *Tonghak* rose again in the south in reaction to the rapid Japanese advance. The rebels were crushed this time, mostly by the Japanese. Leader Chŏn Pongjun was captured and beheaded, and so were countless other rebels. The Japanese were able to easily defeat China and the war came to an end in a treaty in April 1895, in which Japan was granted the island of Taiwan.

The Decline of Chosōn

In the course of the Sino-Japanese War, Japan forced Korea to implement reform by armed threats, while expelling China-oriented conservative politicians from the government. As Japanese encroachment intensified, the Min clique collaborated with Russian Minister Karl Waeber to force the granting of cabinet posts to such pro-Russian people as Yi Pŏmjin.

The government, while reorganizing the military in April 1895, hired Japanese officers as instructors. These officers trained some 800 Korean officers and men who were then assigned to the royal palace as guards under training.

Under these circumstances of doubtful security, the militant Japanese Minister Miura Goro, Secretary

Sugimura, and other Japanese, including Okamoto, decided to assassinate Queen Min, since she was again making secret overtures to China and Russia. Taking advantage of the trainee-guards and those who opposed the Min family, the Japanese troops crushed the resistance offered by the royal body-guards and intruded into Kyŏngbokkung Palace at dawn on October 8, 1895.

Storming into Okhoru Pavilion, the Japanese found and killed Queen Min and then burned her body with kerosene. Foreign missions were outraged by this inhuman atrocity. The Japanese government hurriedly repatriated those involved in the murder and briefly detained them at Hiroshima Prison. Their trial, to borrow the words of Yamabe Kentaro, was "a deliberate miscarriage of justice, designed to protect the culprits."

Despite the Japanese brutality, the European powers, in their apprehension of Russia's southward expansion, acquiesced in the overt Japanese aggression as a counter to the Russian threat. The nation was gripped with indignation at the assassination of Queen Min by a mob of Japanese intruders. Confucian scholars mobilized volunteers to fight against the Japanese.

The history of outright Japanese control in Korea begins with the establishment of the Residency-General on February 1, 1906. The Residency-General was invested with a large measure of competence with regard to Korea's diplomacy, domestic administration and military affairs. Through the Council for Improvement of Korean Administration, the Resident-General forced the Korean government to accept Japan's aggressive policies in every field.

Following his unsuccessful appeal to the American president for help, Emperor Kojong (In August 1897,

King Kojong had crowned himself emperor to symbolize a new beginning as the head of an independent and sovereign state.) sent a party of three men to The Hague in June 1907, where an international peace conference was being held, to seek international support for Korean freedom. Though this support was not forthcoming, Korea's plight gained considerable sympathy abroad as a result. The Japanese were furious and forced Emperor Kojong to abdicate in favor of his son, who was the last monarch of the dynasty and whose posthumous title was Sunjong (r. 1907-1910). Another Korea-Japan agreement was forced upon Korea on July 24 of the same year. It provided a legal basis for Japan's appropriation of Korea's sovereign rights and invested the Resident-General with the principal ruling authority in Korea.

Japanese officials penetrated the executive and judicial branches of the Korean government and the Korean armed forces were disarmed and then disbanded. The Korean Empire had become emasculated. In June 1910, Japan instituted a military police system by appointing the commander of the Japanese military police to the concurrent post of superintendent for police administration.

Korean leaders representing all walks of life committed suicide in opposition to the forced treaty, and many attempts were made to assassinate those ranking officials of the Korean government who had cooperated in bringing the aggressive treaty into being. Korean resistance to Japanese control intensified, but was ruthlessly suppressed by the Japanese military. Uprisings led by Confucian scholars flared in the provinces of Ch'ungch'ŏng-do, Chŏlla-do, Kyŏngsang-do and Kang-won-do.

The resistance assumed major proportions and developed into all-out war against Japan when the regular army joined in the fighting after its forced disbandment by the Japanese. Not only farmers and soldiers, but hunters and workers from northern Korea joined in the resistance: commanders included scholars of the *yangban* class and a number of commoners.

Many pitched battles were fought between 1907 and 1909, but the resistance fighters were more active in guerrilla tactics, rescuing Koreans from Japanese captivity and destroying Japanese transportation and communications facilities. Due to the lack of supplies and weapons, the Korean armed resistance gradually grew weaker, and Japan reported that the Korean volunteer army had ceased to exist in November 1910. At home the resistance took the form of an underground organization, while a group of patriots crossed the Amnokkang and Tuman-gang rivers into Manchuria, where they organized the Korean Independence Army with a stronghold in Kando (Chien-tao).

After 1905, Japanese economic exploitation progressed rapidly. Japanese merchants, supported by generous loans from their home government, controlled the Korean market with huge amounts of capital. The number of Japanese residents in Korea in 1908 was 126,000—by 1911, the number had risen to 210,000. With the enactment of laws conferring extraordinary advantages to the Japanese, Korean farmers fell easy prey to land expropriation and coercive land purchases. The Honam plain, in the Chŏlla-do provinces, long known as the Korean granary, was rapidly becoming a Japanese farm.

The resistance army had grown in strength within its stronghold at Kando in Manchuria. The population of the Kando district as of 1909 consisted of 83,000 Koreans and 21,000 Chinese. Japan embarked on oppression of Korean residents in Kando.

Nevertheless, resistance by Koreans persisted, culminating in the assassination by Ahn Chung-gŭn of former Resident-General Ito at the Harbin Railroad station on October 26, 1909.

Annexation

During the summer of 1910, Japanese Resident-General Terauchi Masatake had a series of secret consultations with Yi Wan-yong, one of the leaders of the powerless Korean government, out of which came the Korea-Japan Annexation Draft. The agreement was signed by Terauchi and Yi and immediately went into force on August 22.

In essence, it provided that the emperor of Korea was to be reduced to king; all treaties between Korea and foreign nations were to become null and void while all treaties between Japan and other nations were to apply to Korea as well; and the Government-General of Korea was to be organized as an agent of the Japanese government to rule the peninsula.

The new Government-General moved first to secure complete control of the populace. Various laws were passed banning political activities and public gatherings. Attempts were made to eradicate Korean national consciousness, in which independence-minded Korean leaders were arrested in thousands, Korean newspapers were banned, hundreds of thousands of copies of books on national heroes or relating to independence were seized and destroyed, and even Korean history was rewritten in a way that would suit their purposes.

The Japanese also tightened their control of traditional as well as private schools, and more than 90 percent of school-age children were denied the opportunity to learn, thereby keeping them illiterate. The 12 years between 1910 and 1922 saw a spectacular decrease in the number of private schools, from more than 2,000 to about 600.

The Independence Movement

The nationwide uprising which broke out on March 1, 1919 was an outcry for national survival in the face of the intolerable aggression, oppression and plundering by the Japanese colonialists. An apparent change in the international situation in the wake of World War I stimulated Korean leaders to intensify the independence struggle, both at home and abroad.

Of the activites abroad, it should be noted that Syngman Rhee, then in the U.S., attempted to participate in the peace conference in Paris in 1918 to make an appeal for Korean independence. His travel abroad was not permitted by the U.S. government, however, which considered its relationship with Japan more important. As an alternative, Rhee made a personal appeal to President Wilson, who was in Paris at that time, to place Korea under the trusteeship of the League of Nations.

At home, leaders of various Korean groups began to cherish the hope that, were the fact of Japanese oppression brought clearly to the attention of a world in which a victorious war had just been fought to end that very sort of tyranny, international pressure would be brought upon Japan, forcing her to relinquish her hold on Korea. A plan was formed. The abdicated Emperor Kojong died in 1919 and his funeral was set for March 3. They decided to take advantage of the occasion and start a nationwide demonstration against Japanese rule on March 1. A Declaration of Independence was drawn up and signed by the 33 leaders of the movement. Copies of this document were secretly printed and circulated throughout the country together with plans for the demonstration.

When the day came, the leaders in Seoul assembled at Pagoda Park and publicly read the declaration which proclaimed to the world that Korea had the right to be a free and independent nation and that Korea had been annexed by Japan unjustly and against the will of its people. Street demonstrations took place all across the country with people carrying the Korean flag, *Taegukki*. The demonstration was peaceful and no violence had been planned.

But, the Japanese reacted with fear and shock. Police fired into unarmed crowds, killing and wounding many. Thousands were arrested, of whom a considerable number died in prison. When this brought attacks on police stations by the angry crowds in some instances, the Japanese retaliated by burning homes and churches, and ruthlessly put down the protest. In all, more than six thousand demonstrators were killed and about 15 thousand wounded. Some 50 thousand others were arrested by the Japanese police.

The March 1 Movement failed to gain the independence for which it was intended. The Japanese were not moved to grant Korea freedom, nor did other nations offer practical support. However, it was of great historic significance as it was the first time that all Koreans, upper and lower class, agreed on a specific goal, and was thus an important means of forging a national consciousness in the modern sense.

Throughout the 1920s and 1930s, resistance to the Japanese became more organized and determined; in return, the cruelly exploitative policies of the colonial administration were made increasingly oppressive. Every part of Korean society became in-

*The 33 leaders of the March 1, 1919
Independence Movement meeting to sign the
Declaration of Independence.*

volved in the struggle: journalists, educators, novelists, poets and religious leaders kept the spiritual flame of independence alive, and among the common people there developed a fierce national pride and determination that was to serve Korea well in the darkest period of its history.

Resistance Against Colonialism

The beginning of Japan's war of aggression on the Asian continent and its spread into the Pacific brought a further tightening of Japan's colonial reins over Korea. The Japanese colonial policy at the time was oriented toward the transformation of Korea into a logistical base for continental aggression. It was the closing phase of Japanese colonial rule in Korea.

Monopolistic capital from Japan flowed into Korea to create the arsenal for an invasion of the continent of China. Moreover, cheap labor was available as the result of Korean impoverishment caused by Japanese exploitation. Rapid advances had been made in some manufacturing, but it was dependent industrialization geared to colonialism.

Japan expanded its war of continental invasion from Manchuria into China proper from July 1937. As war progressed the exploitation of Korean labor became ever greater. Koreans were excluded from positions of skilled work and forced to do merely heavy manual labor at wages less than half those received by their Japanese counterparts. The official enforcement of industrial development went hand in hand with the colonial agricultural policy of increasing rice production. As the tide of war turned against the Japanese, they squeezed more and more agricultural products out of the peasants by means of *kongchul* or "quota delivery."

In March 1944, the Japanese placed production quotas on major mining and manufacturing industries for the purpose of securing military supplies; medium and small enterprises were consolidated. Alignment of colonial industries was undertaken with emphasis placed on iron and light metal industries and production of raw materials. These economic restrictions were accompanied by further infringement upon freedom of thought and civil liberties.

In the course of invading China after 1937, the Japanese began to suppress Koreans' freedom of religion and faith, substituting compulsory worship at Japanese Shinto shrines. In 1938, Korean language teaching was banned from the secondary school curricula according to a new education ordinance, and from April 1941, the curricula of Japanese schools was imposed upon Korean schools. As the war intensified, education of Koreans under the Education Decree of March 1943 was geared to the Japanese war establishment. No longer was Korean language taught in primary school.

But such high-handed oppression by the Japanese Government-General could hardly fail to bring about persistent resistance. Many were arrested on charges of "seeking to attain the ambition of liberating the Korean people." In 1941 a Thought Criminals Preventive Custody Law went into force, and a protective prison was established in Seoul where almost all the anti-Japanese activists were herded. The Government-General declared preventive custody was intended to isolate from society unruly "thought criminals" and to discipline them. It was the first step in a drive to uproot the will to independence from the minds of the Koreans.

In 1942 the Government-General came under the central administrative control of the Japanese government, and a massive mobilization of Korean manpower and materials was integrated into the war effort. From 1943 Korean youths were drafted into the Japanese army, and the Student Volunteer Ordinance of January 20, 1944 forced Korean college students into the army. In accordance with the National General Mobilization Act of Japan, Korean labor was subjected to forcible removal from the peninsula. Drafting of laborers started in 1939 and many were sent to Japan, Sakhalin or to Southeast Asia. Statistics up to August 15, 1945 show that 4,146,098 Korean laborers were forcibly assigned inside Korea and 1,259,933 in Japan alone.

On August 28, 1941, the Korean Provisional Government in China, in response to the declaration by President Roosevelt and Prime Minister Churchill, issued a statement demanding recognition of the Korean government, military, technical and economic assistance for the prosecution of anti-Japanese campaigns, and Korean participation in deciding the fate of Korea after the war.

After Japan's surprise attack on Pearl Harbor in December 1941, the Korean Provisional Government set up a Euro-American Liaison Committee in Washington for the purpose of launching active diplomacy with American and European states. An aid agreement was concluded with the Nationalist Government of China, and efforts were made to strengthen the internal organization of the government. When the Cairo meeting of the U.S., China and Britain (which agreed on the independence of Korea upon Japanese surrender) was scheduled in 1943, Kim Ku of the Provisional Government sought the aid of Chiang Kai-shek, while Liaison Committee Director Syngman Rhee ordered Chŏng Han-gyŏng (Henry Chung) to go to Cairo to promote the cause of Korean independence.

In February 1945, the Provisional Government formally decided to mount more resolute struggles against Japan. In all, about 5,000 Korean youths joined the allied forces in military operations throughout the continental theater of war. They included many of the Korean students forcibly drafted into the Japanese army, who had deserted their units to join the struggles against Japan.

Freed independence fighters who had been imprisoned by Japanese authorities jubilantly ran out of a Seoul prison following national liberation on August 15, 1945.

The Republic of Korea

For Koreans, who had been denied independent development in all walks of life by the Japanese colonial masters, the Japanese surrender was the starting point of other ordeals: that of ideological conflicts similar to those experienced by many postwar colonial peoples, and the problem of how to overcome and liquidate the disastrous consequences of four decades of Japanese domination. In fact, liberation did not bring about full independence for which Koreans had fought so hard, but a partitioned nation.

The occupation of a divided Korea by the United States and the Soviet Union frustrated the efforts of Koreans to establish an independent and unified government, and the transplantation of two divergent political ideologies in the south and the north of the 38th parallel further intensified the national split. In the meantime, among the Allies, the foreign ministers of the United States, Soviet Russia and Britain met in Moscow on December 15, 1945 and decided to put Korea under the trusteeship of the four great powers (the U.S., the USSR, Britain, and China) as a provisional step to unite the divided country. The nation protested against the international decision imposed upon Korea only four months after liberation from colonial rule. The Moscow decision cast a shadow over Korean hopes for establishment of an independent government.

Although the Communists decided to support the Moscow decision by order from the USSR, the vast majority of the people determinedly opposed trusteeship as another form of alien domination. This problem, together with that of ideologies, further accelerated the national split.

The partitioned occupation of Korea by the United

States and Soviet Russia caused internal conflicts detrimental to the efforts for independence. The series of postwar international decisions made in disregard of the Korean people left them far from the goal of national independence.

The internal disorder south of the 38th parallel worsened in proportion to the rigid regimentation of society under the Communist system in the north until 1948, when two ideologically opposed governments were established. The government of the Republic of Korea was established on August 15 and took over control from the U.S. Military Government.

The new government faced the pressing task of rebuilding the faltering and heavily-exploited economy. This, together with all the various problems, was too comprehensive to be considered mere postwar phenomena. The ideological confrontation between the North and South inevitably engendered a tense military confrontation, and this was another major burden placed on the government.

In 1949 the United States withdrew its occupation forces from Korea, leaving only a small group of military advisers. The Soviet Union also pulled its forces out of northern Korea, but only after setting up in the North a well-trained and equipped army. North Korea was also in military alliance with the Chinese Communists who had just swept across the Chinese mainland.

The Korean War

Early on the morning of June 25, 1950, without any warning or declaration of war, masses of North Korean troops crossed the 38th parallel and swept down upon an unprepared South. The Republic's troops fought bravely, but proved no match for the heavily armed Communists and their Russian T-34 tanks. Seoul fell in three days and almost all of South Korea was overrun in about a month with the defenders penned up in a small corner in the southeast known as the "Pusan perimeter."

The Republic of Korea immediately appealed to the United Nations. In response, the Security Council passed a resolution demanding the Communists withdraw to the 38th parallel and encouraging all member nations to give military support to the Republic. United States troops soon began to arrive, and were subsequently joined by those of 15 other nations. Under the command of General Douglas MacArthur they began to reverse the trend of the war, and after a surprise landing at Inch'ŏn pushed the Communists out of South Korea and advanced into the North. Some units reached the Amnokkang River, and it seemed unification would at last be realized.

But in October the Communist Chinese intervened. Chinese troops appeared in such large numbers that the U.N. forces were compelled to make a strategic retreat, and Seoul once again fell into Communist hands on January 4, 1951. The U.N. forces regrouped and mounted a counterattack retaking Seoul on March 12. A stalemate was reached roughly in the area along the 38th parallel, where the conflict had begun.

At this point the Russians called for truce negotiations, which finally began at Kaesŏng in July 1951 and were transferred to P'anmunjŏm in November of the same year. These talks dragged on for over two years before a cease-fire agreement was finally reached on July 27, 1953.

The combat casualties of the three-year war numbered 147,000 South Korean troops, 35,000 U.N. troops, 520,000 North Korean troops and 900,000

Red Chinese soldiers. Non-military casualties in South Korea reached 245,000 killed and 230,000 injured in battle-related action. In addition, 330,000 were listed as missing, 130,000 killed in Communist atrocities and 85,000 forcibly taken to North Korea. The police death toll numbered 16,000.

Democratic Revolution—Rhee's Downfall

In the aftermath of the war, not only economic but very serious social and political problems appeared. These mainly centered around the Liberal Party regime of President Syngman Rhee. The old patriot, unable to see that he had outlived his usefulness, clung tenaciously to power. Rhee and his associates refused to let democratic processes take their normal course.

Social disorders and hostility to the government complicated the already staggering social problems created by the war. There were some 300,000 war-widows, over 100,000 orphans, and hundreds of thousands of unemployed, whose numbers swelled by farmers leaving their land to seek work in the cities. Exact statistics are not available, but in 1961 it was estimated that there were about 279,000 unemployed, of whom 72,000 were university graduates and 51,000 were discharged soldiers and laid-off workers. Here was a powder keg of anger and resentment that waited only for a spark to set it off.

The spark was provided by President Rhee and his Liberal Party in the course of the elections of 1960. Realizing its unpopularity, the Liberal Party used every means at its disposal to rig the elections. Demonstrations broke out almost at once, especially among students. On the evening of the election day, March 15, in Masan near Pusan, thousands of citizens and students marched through the streets, protesting election rigging. Police fired on the crowds, killing eight and wounding some 50 others. About 20 days later, the remains of a high school student who had been reported missing since the election-day demonstration were found along the shore of Masan; a tear gas canister was studded in the skull. This triggered fresh waves of demonstrations.

Demonstrations, largely by students, flared up in almost all major cities, climaxing in Seoul on April 19 when hundreds of thousands of students from nearly all colleges and high schools hit the streets. The government proclaimed martial law. Nevertheless, protest demonstrations continued.

President Rhee finally yielded and announced his resignation on April 27. A caretaker government was promptly organized, led by Huh Chŏng, one-time prime minister, which managed new general elections that gave a landslide victory to the theretofore opposition Democratic Party. Though victorious, the Democrats were beset with serious intraparty factionalism. The grabbing of power and the long-brewing strife between "new" and "old" factions, virtually split the party into two.

Under the revised Constitution that adopted a cabinet system instead of the presidential system, the new National Assembly in August elected Rep. Yun Po-sun from the "old" faction for the rather ceremonial post of President and Rep. Chang Myŏn of the "new" faction as Prime Minister. The new government, however, was not capable of coping with the confusion that ensued. People, long controlled by an authoritarian regime, seemed to think they could get overnight everything they wanted now that the ironfisted regime had gone. Over-confident students who had just toppled a regime were attempting to sway the conduct of national affairs. Chang's cabinet, badly weakened by the intraparty split, was simply helpless against endless daily demonstrations.

To compound the situation, the North Korean Communists, having recovered from the almost suicidal adventure of 1950-53, seized the golden opportunity of internal disorder in the South following Rhee's downfall to subvert whatever effort the Chang administration could put forth. Elements of doubtful allegiance began mouthing "Peaceful Unification"— that familiar line of propaganda which was emanating from Radio P'yŏngyang day in and day out at that time.

Military Revolution

Before daybreak on May 16, 1961, a group of military officers under the leadership of Major General Park Chung Hee staged a bloodless coup. Later in the morning, the Military Revolution Committee, headed by Army Chief of Staff Lt. General Chang To-yŏng, announced over the radio that it had taken over all three branches of the government and proclaimed a six-point pledge—strong anti-Communism, respect for the U.N. Charter, closer relations with the United States and other free nations, eradication of corruption, establishment of a self-supporting economy, efforts for national reunification, and transfer of the government to civilian rule as soon as the revolutionary missions were accomplished.

On the afternoon of May 18, Dr. Chang appeared in the Capitol Building and held his last cabinet meeting. As a result, he issued a radio message announcing his resignation as prime minister and assuming political and moral responsibility for the situation leading to the military revolution. The outgoing cabinet also approved martial law, which was forwarded to President Yun, who formally proclaimed it. In this way, transfer of government from Chang Myŏn to the Revolutionary Committee was made within the legal framework of the Constitution.

The Third and Fourth Republics

As promised, the Revolutionary Committee composed of military officers, later renamed the Supreme Council for National Reconstruction, gradually made arrangements to restore civilian rule. In December 1963 the Third Republic was inaugurated under the leadership of President Park Chung Hee, then a civilian, who was elected as the head of state in a general election. President Park was reelected in 1967 and 1971. This period was highlighted by rapid economic advance, normalization of relations with Japan, and the active expansion of diplomatic relations throughout the world.

On the Korean peninsula, the first contact between the South and the North in the quarter-century history of national division was made in 1971. At the suggestion of the South, Red Cross officials from the two sides began to meet in August 1971 on the issue of reuniting separated families. A joint communique was released on July 4, 1972 in which the two sides promised cooperative efforts to achieve peaceful unification. The South-North Coordinating Committee was formed under the communique and met in Seoul and P'yŏngyang by turn.

By 1972, things were looking quite hopeful for Korea, but there were dangers just under the surface of events which had to be faced. While Korea was doing well economically, it still was a developing country. Though there was great euphoria over the commencement of negotiations with North Korea, the risks were realized to be great and the chances of success slim. The leader of North Korea, Kim Il-sung, could not be expected to negotiate if there were any signs that he could unite the country unilaterally and by force on his own terms. The ROK had to be strong, united and vigilant. Furthermore, power relations in East Asia were also shifting in 1972. The strength of Japan, the increasing international acceptance of the People's Republic of China and the lessening of America's role in the defense of Asian countries were realities that could not be avoided.

In short, during 1972 Korea faced a new international and security situation on top of the need to strengthen the economy. President Park felt it was time to revise the Constitution to give the president sufficient power to meet potential crises with speed and resolve. The Yushin (Revitalizing Reforms) Constitution was approved in a nationwide plebiscite, inaugurating the Fourth Republic in December 1972. New presidential and National Assembly elections were held.

In the ensuing years, Korea successfully weathered the oil crisis and continued to grow. The *Saemaŭl* Movement brought increasing prosperity to rural and urban areas and provided experience in democratic problem-solving, and diplomatic relations continued to expand. Only the South-North dialogue floundered and then came to a standstill.

Tragically, on October 26, 1979, President Park Chung Hee was struck down by an assassin's bullet. Prime Minister Choi Kyu Hah became acting president according to the Constitution, and was shortly thereafter elected president by the National Council for Unification, an electoral college set up as part of the Yushin system.

During the next several months, Korea went through a difficult period of soul-searching and adjustment to the post-Park era, characterized by political, social and economic instability. Out of this seemingly chaotic situation, there emerged a consensus that there must be a new constitution fitting the new political leadership. A more sophisticated citizenry was entering a new decade with vastly different problems and needs than Korea had faced in the 1970s. There was also agreement that in spite of the great success in development, there had been a number of negative side effects which needed immediate reform if Korea was to regain lost momentum and revive creativity.

During this period of transition, General Chun Doo Hwan emerged as the dominant leader of the nation; directing the reform movement, restoring order and setting new priorities for the government. On August 16, 1980, President Choi resigned, citing the need to make the transition period as short as possible. General Chun resigned from the Army on August 22 and was elected president by the National Conference for Unification on August 27.

Immediate social and economic reforms were set in motion, and in October, the President promulgated a new constitution, approved by popular vote, guaranteeing political and civil rights and limiting the presidency to a single seven-year term.

The Fifth Republic

President Chun set four goals for the Fifth Republic: to cultivate the type of democracy best suited to the political climate of Korea, to promote the welfare of all citizens to the greatest possible extent, to uphold justice in all areas of national life, and to bring about spiritual reform by revamping the educational system and developing higher standards of culture.

Events leading up to the establishment of the Fifth Republic were swift. Following the promulgation of the new constitution, political parties began organizational activities in December 1980, and all political activities were resumed in January 1981. In February, the electoral college and presidential elections were held, in which President Chun was re-elected with overwhelming support. A month later general elections held for the National Assembly also gave a landslide victory to the Democratic Justice Party, led by President Chun.

The first achievement of the new government was to effect a change in public attitudes and release a new creative energy. Following the assassination of President Park, a pall seemed to descend over the country, compounded by political and social unrest, rising oil prices and a poor harvest. However, after only a few months, the determination and hard work of the people began once more to pay handsomely in social, economic and political dividends.

Diplomatically, Korea has begun to take an increasingly active role more appropriate to its economic and political vitality. In January 1981, President Chun invited North Korea's Kim Il-sung to visit South Korea in the hope that such a move would break the stalemate in South-North relations. On January 28, the President left for the United States on a 10-day state visit during which the two allies renewed their friendship and agreed to strengthen economic and security ties.

In late June and early July 1981, President Chun made state visits to the five ASEAN countries to further cement amicable ties, stressing the importance of cooperation and solidarity among Pacific-basin

nations for the unfolding of a great Pacific era. Again in August 1982, President Chun toured four African countries—Kenya, Nigeria, Gabon and Senegal—and Canada. Being the first Korean president ever to visit Africa, President Chun called for "South-South cooperation" among developing countries as a means of better coping with universal economic difficulties.

A scheduled trip to six nations in Southwest Asia and Oceania was abruptly cancelled in October 1983, when North Korea bombed the presidential delegation in Rangoon, Burma in a nearly successful attempt to assassinate President Chun. The atrocity, however, was not able to dampen Korea's increasingly productive relations with these nations nor to put an end to the President's persistent pressure on North Korea to seek a rational solution to the division of the nation.

In a state visit to Japan in September 1984, the first for a Korean head of state, President Chun received an expression of regret from Emperor Hirohito for past Japanese colonial occupation. The meeting is seen as the opening of a new era of friendship with Japan.

In April 1985, President Chun made a second trip to the United States in what has become a more or less regular meeting with the President of the nation's closest ally. Then in the following April, the President went to Great Britain, Germany, France and Belgium, signalling a broadening of Korea's foreign policy interests to include a new emphasis on the Atlantic nations. As a result of these and other meetings with world leaders in Seoul and of the growth of Korea as an economic power and a world trading nation, Korea is rapidly approaching the status of a middle power with considerable world influence.

In a mid-air conference on the flight from Washington to Honolulu, President Chun said that the most important outcome of the summit conference with President Reagan was their timely agreement on the need to strengthen security arrangements for Korea.   85

Seoul, the center of government, will host the 1988 Summer Olympics.

Constitution

Constitutional History

The Constitution of the Republic of Korea was first promulgated on July 17, 1948. The constituent National Assembly formed that year through a United Nations-supervised election had adopted the Constitution on July 12, 1948, setting the base for the first democratic republic on the Korean peninsula.

In 1947 the United Nations General Assembly had resolved that general elections should be conducted throughout Korea under United Nations supervision to establish a unified government. The United Nations Temporary Commission on Korea (UNTCOK) was thus to supervise peninsula-wide elections to form that government, at which time both the USSR and U.S. forces were to withdraw.

The seeds of tragedy were sown when the Soviets refused UNTCOK entry to supervise elections in the region north of the 38th parallel. When it became apparent that the Soviet refusal was intractable, the decision was made to honor the U.N. resolution as far as possible by holding elections in the part of Korea accessible to the UNTCOK. On May 10, 1948, Korean voters elected 198 representatives to the National Assembly, leaving 100 seats vacant in case elections were later held in the North.

Taehan Min-guk, the Republic of Korea, was adopted as the official name of the nation on May 31 in the National Assembly's first session. The representatives then went to work on drafting a constitution, which was adopted on July 12 and promulgated on July 17. A president was elected under the provisions of that Constitution and a government immediately formed. On August 15, 1948, the third anniversary of national liberation, the Republic of Korea was proclaimed to the world.

The Constitution and the various governments of the Republic of Korea were to be severely tested in the years to come. In September 1948, in defiance of the U.N. resolution and in violation of their wartime agreement on occupation as a temporary administrative measure, the Soviet forces presided over the creation of a Communist regime north of the 38th parallel. Propaganda assaults, guerrilla raids and subversion directed against the Republic of Korea began almost immediately, ultimately resulting in the invasion of the Republic of Korea by Soviet-equipped North Korean forces on June 25, 1950. More than three years later, the Korean War ended with an armistice agreement signed at the truce village of P'anmunjŏm on July 27, 1953.

But the division of the peninsula roughly along the 38th parallel and the bellicosity of the North Korean Communists remain. These factors continue to exert strong influence on the constitutional development of the Republic of Korea. In a search for the proper balance among the three branches of government—the executive, the legislative and the judicial—that would facilitate the nation's development and secure its existence, the Constitution has undergone eight amendments: on July 7, 1952 and November 29, 1954 during the First Republic; on June 15 and November 29, 1960 during the Second Republic; on December 26, 1962 and October 21, 1969 during the Third Republic; and on December 27, 1972, forming the Fourth Republic. Most recently, on October 27, 1980, the Korean people approved by popular referendum the eighth amendment to the Constitution, creating the Fifth Republic, in the wake of the assassination of President Park Chung Hee on October 26, 1979.

To preclude any repetition of those unfortunate events, a Constitutional Amendment Deliberation

Council was established March 14, 1980, under the direct authority of the President, to study and develop a draft constitution. The imperatives defined by the Council were to cultivate the form of democracy best suited for the political climate in Korea, to promote the welfare of all citizens to the greatest possible extent, to firmly uphold justice in all areas of national life, and to bring about a spiritual reform by revamping the educational system and developing higher cultural standards.

The most noteworthy of these goals and the general governmental structure defined by the Constitution of the Fifth Republic of Korea are examined in the following sections.

Highlights of the
Fifth Republic Constitution

The drafting of the Constitution for the Fifth Republic officially began January 20, 1980, when the government organized a constitution study group of 30 experts recruited from various walks of life. The study group developed basic concepts and directions for a constitutional revision after about two months of study. The Constitutional Amendment Deliberation Council, established March 14, 1980, developed a draft constitution. Chaired by the Prime Minister, the Council was composed of 69 members from political, academic, business, legal, journalistic and other diverse social circles.

Opinions on how to rewrite the constitution were solicited from a large number of people from all walks of life and were reflected in the draft constitution to a considerable extent. When members of the Council disagreed on specific topics, representatives of interested organizations and staff experts were invited to present their views. The bill revising the Constitution was completed in late September 1980. On October 22, 1980, 95.1 percent of the eligible voters turned out to vote in a constitutional referendum, and 91.6 percent of those voting endorsed the amended constitution.

The revised Constitution outlines a political system founded on the ideals of liberal democracy. Innovative institutional devices were adopted to assure the nation's survival and security and to eliminate entrenched elements of inefficiency from the management of state affairs. The revised Constitution also expressly strengthens the Republic of Korea's commitment to a just and democratic state under the principles of a free economy, and to fostering Korea's unique national traditions and cultural heritage.

The Constitution of the Fifth Republic provides for a presidential system designed to achieve the strong and effective leadership essential to national security, as well as political and social stability, in an atmosphere of national unity and harmony. At the same time, the Constitution reinforces the inviolability of basic human rights, and upholds the principle of checks and balances in government by restricting presidential powers, strengthening the functions of the legislature and ensuring the independence of the judiciary.

Especially noteworthy are safeguard provisions that ensure peaceful changes of government and prevent anyone from holding the reins of government for an overly long period. More specifically, these provisions ensure free competition in presidential races in a clean political atmosphere and limit presidential tenure to a single seven-year term. These provisions not only mark a milestone in Korea's constitutional history, but also embody a bold and conscious affirmation of democratic politics with few parallels in modern times.

Essentially, the Constitution of the Fifth Republic aims at an optimal harmony of the national ideals of security, order and efficiency with the people's call for democratization, while guaranteeing human rights to the greatest possible extent. This harmony is achieved by stressing the inviolability of basic rights, so that a just and democratic society dedicated to the well-being of all its citizens can materialize without fail.

The *habeas corpus* system, abolished in the Fourth Republic, is a key provision in the present Constitution. "Guilt by relation," wherein the relatives of those convicted of certain types of offenses suffered unfavorable treatment with respect to employment or permission to travel abroad, has been eliminated.

The freedoms of speech, press, assembly and association are explicitly guaranteed; conversely, social responsibility in exercising the freedoms of speech and the press are prescribed, as is redress for those who suffer from the irresponsible exercise of the same by others. Confessions under duress are declared unacceptable as evidence, and no conviction may be made when a confession is the only evidence.

Workers' rights to independent association, collective bargaining and collective action are more explicitly guaranteed, although it is still recognized that in some fields these rights must yield priority to national interests. The rights to happiness, a clean environment and

The National Assembly in session. The Assembly is composed of 276 members, 184 elected by popular vote and 92 appointed by the parties in proportion to the percentage of the seats won in the election.

privacy, and the right to be considered innocent until proven guilty are also explicitly guaranteed, along with protection from *ex post facto* arrest.

The Executive

The Constitution provides for indirect presidential elections through an electoral college elected by secret popular vote and composed of no less than 5,000 delegates, with the exact number to be determined by law. A presidential candidate may either be nominated by a political party or recommended by a certain number of electoral college delegates, a number which is also determined by law.

A delegate to the electoral college is permitted to affiliate himself with a political party and cannot be arrested or detained except in cases of *flagrante delicto*. Members of the National Assembly and other public officials may not become electoral college delegates, nor may delegates run in the first National Assembly election conducted after they serve as members of the college.

The electoral college is dissolved when the term of the president elected by it begins. When the office of president is vacated, a new electoral college is formed within three months to choose a successor to serve for a full seven-year term.

The term of office of the president is seven years, and no one may become president for a second term. If a future constitutional amendment should be enacted to extend the term of office of the president or to permit the president to serve more than one term, such an amendment will not be applicable to the president in office at the time of the proposal. These provisions form a double safeguard against anyone seizing the reins of government power for a protracted period.

During the Fourth Republic, the president was empowered to take emergency measures not only when national security or public safety was threatened, but also when such a threat was anticipated. The revised Constitution does not provide for such a "precautionary" exercise of presidential emergency powers.

The Fourth Republic Constitution required the president to merely notify the National Assembly of emergency measures taken, whereas the present Constitution provides that emergency measures taken by the president are nullified if they are not approved by the National Assembly. In addition, the president is required to lift emergency measures when so requested by the National Assembly.

Whereas the previous Constitution gave the president the unconditional prerogative to dissolve the National Assembly, the Fifth Republic Constitution empowers him to do so only after consultation with the Assembly Speaker and deliberations at the State Council, and when there are reasons to deem it necessary for the sake of "the security of the State and the interests of all the people." It further provides that the National Assembly may not be dissolved within one year of its formation and that it may not be dissolved twice for the same reason. The previous presidential prerogative to nominate one-third of the members of the National Assembly has been abolished. A further adjustment of checks and balances in government is found in the provision empowering the president to appoint the chief justice of the Supreme Court with the consent of the National Assembly, and justices of the Supreme Court on the recommendation of the chief

STATE STRUCTURE OF
THE REPUBLIC OF KOREA

```
Legislature  <-->  President  <-->  Judiciary
                       |
                  Prime Minister
```

Economic Planning Board	Ministry of Government Administration	Ministry of Science and Technology	National Unification Board	Minister of State for Political Affairs	Office of Legislation	Patriots and Veterans Affairs Agency
Ministry of Foreign Affairs	Ministry of Home Affairs	Ministry of Finance	Ministry of Justice	Ministry of National Defense	Ministry of Education	Ministry of Sports	Ministry of Agriculture and Fisheries
Ministry of Trade and Industry	Ministry of Energy and Resources	Ministry of Construction	Ministry of Health and Social Affairs	Ministry of Labor Affairs	Ministry of Transportation	Ministry of Communications	Ministry of Culture and Information

justice, rather than the previous presidential prerogative of appointing all judges.

The president functions not only as head of the Executive Branch in domestic affairs, but also as the head of state in foreign relations. He has the express constitutional duty of pursuing the peaceful unification of the country. He is the chairman of the State Council (cabinet) as well as commander-in-chief of the Armed Forces. He has the power to appoint or relieve the prime minister and cabinet ministers, heads of government agencies and offices, ambassadors, provincial governors and other senior public officials. He has the power to conclude treaties, accredit or dispatch diplomatic envoys; and declare war or conclude peace. He may also grant amnesty, commutation and the restoration of civil rights to convicted felons.

The Legislature

With the adoption of the Fifth Republic Constitution, two-thirds of the members of the National Assembly of the Republic of Korea are elected by popular vote to a term of four years. The total number of Assembly members provided by the Constitution is no less than 200, with the exact number to be determined by law. A proportional representation system, aimed at encouraging legislative participation through political parties by people from all walks of life, is provided in the Constitution, with the specifics to be determined by law.

The powers of the National Assembly were extended in the Fifth Republic Constitution in order to improve the checks and balances in the Korean government.

The parliamentary right to inspect government operations is recognized in the Constitution, as is the right to vote nonconfidence in the prime minister or an individual cabinet minister, though the right to demand dismissal of the prime minister—which entails the dismissal of the cabinet *en masse*—may not be exercised within one year of his confirmation by the National Assembly.

The National Assembly's role in constitutional amendments was greatly expanded by the Fifth Republic Constitution. Regardless of whether an amendment is sponsored by the National Assembly or the president, it is first subject to approval by the National Assembly and then to a national referendum for enactment.

On the other hand, the Constitution contains provisions aimed at improving the conduct and qualifications of National Assembly members. It expressly requires that they maintain high standards of integrity and that they place the national interest before all other considerations. A previous ban on extra-Assembly remunerative activities was found to have abetted influence-peddling practices. Therefore, the Fifth Republic Constitution permits such remunerative activities for National Assembly members, with the exception of a few categories specified by law.

Major functions of the National Assembly, aside from those outlined above, include the power to deliberate and propose, and approve or reject legislative bills, to finalize and inspect closing accounts of the national budget, to ratify or reject foreign treaties, and to concur in the declaration of war or conclusion of peace.

The Judiciary

The highest tribunal in the country, the Supreme Court examines and passes final decisions on appeals against the decisions of appellate courts in civil and criminal cases. Its decisions are final and indisputable, forming judicial precedents. The chief justice is appointed by the president to a single five-year term with the consent of the National Assembly, and justices of the Supreme Court are appointed by the president upon the recommendation of the chief justice. The previous Constitution empowered the president to appoint all judges without restraints from the other branches of government. The present Constitution empowers the chief justice to appoint judges to all lower courts to better guarantee the independence of the judiciary.

Greater security is given to judicial posts in the present Constitution. Previously, judges could be dismissed by administrative action by the chief executive. That provision was deleted from the Fifth Republic Constitution, which provides that a judge may be dismissed only by criminal proceedings or impeachment. The functioning of the Supreme Court is strengthened in the present Constitution by allowing the appointment of judges, in addition to justices, as well as the establishment of special departments at the Supreme Court for such fields as public administration, taxes, labor and military matters.

Inter-Korean Relations

A lookout point at the Military Demarcation Zone.

Initial Efforts for Unification

Various attempts to unify Korea have been made since the country was divided at the end of World War II in 1945. But all of them failed due to the intransigence of the Communists—initially the occupying Soviets and later the North Koreans were interested only in the communization of all of Korea.

The initial effort was exerted between the U.S. and Soviet occupation forces in 1946. Earlier, in December 1945, the foreign ministers of the U.S., Great Britain and the Soviet Union met in Moscow and agreed among other things, to have the occupation forces in Korea help the Koreans form a unified provisional government. Acting under the Moscow protocol, the U.S. and Soviet commands formed a Joint U.S.-USSR Commission, which met in Seoul from March-May 1946 and again from May-October 1947.

But the Joint Commission failed to produce any solution due to wide differences in the two countries' basic positions. The crux of the failure was the Soviet attempt to exclude rightist Korean leaders from the formation of a unified government. Their underlying policy was that they would not cooperate in realizing Korean unification unless it was achieved under Communism. Upon the final breakup of the Joint Commission in October 1947, the United States decided to refer the Korean question to the newly inaugurated United Nations.

On November 14, 1947, the U.N. General Assembly adopted a resolution stipulating that general elections be held on the entire Korean peninsula to establish a unified government and that a temporary commission be formed to observe general elections. The U.N. Temporary Commission arrived in Seoul in January 1948 but the Soviets in the North blocked the entry of the

North and South Korean relatives had an opportunity to meet each other for the first time in more than 30 years on September 20-23, 1985.

U.N. Commission into North Korea.

Here, the Interim Committee of the U.N. General Assembly resolved that if supervision in all areas of the Korean peninsula was impossible, the Commission should observe elections in areas where it can have access. As a result, general elections were held only in South Korea in May 1948 under U.N. supervision, thus letting go a rare opportunity to form a unified government.

Another futile attempt was mounted upon the cease-fire of the Korean War. The Armistice Agreement signed in July 1953 to end the three-year war provided, among other things, for a high-level conference among countries involved to determine the political future of Korea. The representatives of the Republic of Korea and 16 U.N. Korean War allies and the delegates from the Soviet Union, the People's Republic of China and North Korea met in Geneva in April 1954. However, the meeting broke up in June the same year, with the Communist side refusing to accept the competence and authority of the United Nations and seeking ways to communize all Korea.

With the rupture of the Geneva conference, the duty of handling the Korean question reverted to the United Nations. The world organization debated the Korean question, reaffirming its call for unification achieved through U.N.-supervised general elections in all Korea, until the mid-1970s when it stopped taking up the Korean issue in the belief that less constructive debates would only fan unnecessary confrontation between the two ideological camps.

South-North Dialogue

As international efforts to solve the question of Korea had faltered, the government of the Republic of Korea resolved to take the matter in its own hands. The government was convinced that discussion between the direct parties concerned would be the shortest route to bringing about a solution. In a Liberation Day address on August 15, 1970, President Park Chung Hee implicitly heralded his project of initiating a direct inter-Korean dialogue. Challenging North Korea to accept a "peaceful competition of good will," pending unification, President Park said he was considering some drastic measures to solve humanitarian problems and gradually tear down the artificial barrier between the two sides of Korea.

One of the measures came one year later when the Republic of Korea National Red Cross proposed to the North Korean Red Cross on August 12, 1971 a South-North Red Cross meeting on the issue of reuniting the families dispersed between the two sides of Korea. North Korea agreed and the two Red Cross societies began holding preliminary contacts at P'anmunjŏm in September 1971.

But the preliminary talks soon stalemated as the North Korean Red Cross began to inject politics into the supposedly humanitarian business. The Republic of Korea, believing some political breakthrough was necessary, let it be known to North Korea that it was ready to open a separate political dialogue. P'yŏng-yang responded affirmatively, and there ensued secret contacts, including trips to P'yŏngyang and Seoul by southern and northern emissaries. The culmination came on July 4, 1972 when the two sides simultaneously issued the South-North Joint Communique, in which they pledged to improve mutual understanding, remove mistrust, ease tensions and expedite national unification through dialogue and other peaceful means.

Under the Joint Communique, the South and the North formed the South-North Coordinating Committee to enter political contacts. It also served to spur the business of the Red Cross talks. The dialogue at the two channels seemed to be going smoothly, holding sessions in Seoul and P'yŏngyang alternately for a while. Before long, in early 1973, however, North Korea started to apply a brake to the talks, posing unacceptable conditions such as the repeal of the anti-Communism policy and withdrawal of U.S. forces from Korea. Finally, on August 28, 1973, North Korea

*The 8th round of inter-Korean Red Cross
talks to arrange family reunions was held*

Major Indices of South and North Korea

(As of 1984)

	Unit	South Korea	North Korea
Population	1,000	40,578	19,323
Population Growth Rate	%	1.55	2.23
Economically Active Population	1,000	14,984	8,600
Area	Km²	99,117	122,098
GNP*	US$ billion	81.1	14.7

*Based on current prices.

in Seoul on May 28-29, 1985 after a 13-year hiatus.

	Unit	South Korea	North Korea
Per Capita GNP	US$	1,998	762
Real Growth Rate	%	7.5	3.9
Ratio of Military Spending to GNP	%	5.8	23.5
Merchandise Exports	US$ billion	29.2	1.3
Merchandise Imports	US$ billion	30.6	1.4

abruptly announced that it would boycott any further inter-Korean meetings.

The Republic of Korea mounted a new initiative in November 1973 to resume the suspended dialogue. As a result, a series of meetings between the vice-chairmen of the Coordinating Committee began to take place at P'anmunjŏm and so did Red Cross delegates' contacts, later replaced with working-level meetings, in December and November 1973, respectively. But these preliminary talks failed to produce any progress with the North Koreans holding fast to their absurd conditions. Apparently believing that the contacts weren't in the interests of the Communist cause, P'yŏngyang put off indefinitely the vice-chairmen's meeting on May 29, 1975 and the Red Cross working-level contacts on March 19, 1978.

As 1979 began amidst a complete standstill in inter-Korean talks, the Republic of Korea endeavored earnestly to resume the dialogue. On January 19, 1979, President Park called on North Korea to agree to resume the suspended talks between responsible authorities at any place, any time and at any level. North Korea responded favorably but in the name of an unofficial organization. A rather abnormal meeting ensued between a delegation from the Seoul side of the South-North Coordinating Committee and northern delegates, representatives of an unofficial organization, the "Democratic Front for Unification of the Fatherland." But, even this meeting didn't last long. North Korean delegates failed to show up at a working-level delegates meeting on March 28, 1979 as proposed by the Seoul side of the Coordinating Committee.

It was obvious that North Korea, which had accepted the dialogue originally with the hope of using it as a means of subverting the Republic of Korea, broke it off as it realized that the talks would not serve that purpose. The same was true of the North Korean call for a prime ministers meeting.

In January 1980 when the Republic of Korea plunged into social confusion in the wake of the sudden demise of President Park in October 1979, North Korea proposed a meeting between the prime ministers of the two sides, obviously in response to the earlier call by President Choi Kyu Hah on North Korea to agree to any of the previous Seoul proposals to resume dialogue. A series of working-level contacts designed to prepare for the proposed prime ministers meeting took place at P'anmunjŏm before North Korea broke it off in September 1980 upon the restoration of stability in the South under the leadership of President Chun Doo Hwan.

Very little progress was made in South-North dialogue after that until President Chun proposed, on August 20, 1984, the early initiation of South-North trade and economic cooperation, offering free technological and commodity assistance, to end the confrontation and open up an era of reconciliation. This seemed to have fallen on deaf ears but in September, North Korea suddenly offered to provide relief goods to flood victims in the South. The South, in what has been widely described as a "surprise move," decided to accept the offer in the hope it would break the ice, which, indeed, it seemed to do.

In the following month, preliminary contacts were begun to revive the Plenary South-North Red Cross Conference on the reunion of separated families, after a 12-year hiatus, and also by the initiation of trade and economic talks. By early September 1985, three sessions of economic talks had taken place at the truce village of P'anmunjŏm. Plenary Red Cross conference meetings were held in Seoul and P'yŏngyang alternately, leading to an agreement to exchange home visiting groups and performing art troupes at the end of the month. Furthermore, two working-level inter-Korean meetings had been held to discuss the North Korean proposal for a South-North inter-parliamentary conference.

In spite of the gradual resumption of South-North contacts, few concrete results had been achieved by September 1985. While past experience forbids any premature optimism and there is always the possibility that North Korea will break off contacts at any time, there are also signs that at least in the short term, the North finds the dialogue again to its advantage. The South, on its part, will continue to work in the hope that real progress can be made to reduce tension and bring about real reconciliation as a basis for peace and eventual unification.

Policy Announcements and Proposals

The basic stand of the Republic of Korea toward the inter-Korean question is that peace should be ensured first on the Korean peninsula with the two sides of Korea engaging in mutual exchanges and cooperation starting in non-sensitive and practicable areas. The Republic believes that by so doing, the two sides could broaden the horizon of understanding, leading to national reconciliation and ultimately to peaceful unification. This policy has been envisaged in a series of policy announcements and proposals.

Special Statement Regarding Foreign Policy: On June 23, 1973, the government issued the Special Statement Regarding Foreign Policy for Peace and Unification with a view to effectively coping with worldwide trends toward detente and better facilitating inter-Korean talks. The policy statement said the Republic of Korea would not object to North Korea's joining international organizations along with the South pending the time of unification, and would open its door to all countries on a reciprocal basis regardless of their ideologies and systems. It also stressed the importance of accomplishing unification by peaceful means, calling for continued efforts to secure concrete results from the inter-Korean dialogue.

Proposal for a Non-Aggression Agreement: The government proposed on January 18, 1974 that a non-aggression agreement be concluded between the South and the North of Korea as a means of ensuring lasting peace on the Korean peninsula. The proposal said that the two sides would, in the suggested agreement, renounce invasion of the other side, refrain from interfering in each other's internal affairs, and see to it that the existing Armistice Agreement remain in force. The proposal was considered most realistic and practical, for, since no peaceful unification is achievable in a short span of time under the circumstances, the best thing for both sides to do is to coexist peacefully, expanding dialogue and exchanges, thereby laying a groundwork for peaceful unification.

Three Principles for Peaceful Unification: On August 15, 1974, the government declared the Three Basic Principles for Peaceful Unification, stipulating 1) peace should be firmly established on the Korean peninsula, 2) the two sides should open their doors to each other through constructive dialogue, exchanges and cooperation, and 3) unification should be achieved through free general elections held under fair management and in direct proportion to the indigenous population. Those principles clearly represent the Republic's basic policy.

Proposals for Visits and a Meeting between Top Leaders: In a bid to break the deadlock of inter-Korean dialogue, President Chun Doo Hwan on January 12, 1981, extended an invitation to North Korea's Kim Il-sung to visit Seoul free of any obligation on his part, and expressed his willingness to go to North Korea on the same terms if invited. It was hoped that such a firsthand experience would help to eradicate the vast areas of misinformation which act as a stumbling block to mutual understanding. Again on June 5 the same year, President Chun proposed to meet Kim Il-sung at any time and any place chosen by P'yŏngyang to discuss any issues raised by either side. Also in the proposal, President Chun advocated that both sides open their societies to the entire Korean people who, he said, have the right to make decisions concerning unification. The offer represented the President's strong desire to realize peaceful unification by prompting North Korea to abandon their dream of communizing all Korea by force of arms.

Formula for National Reconciliation and Democratic Unification: On January 22, 1982, President Chun Doo Hwan made public a more systematic and comprehensive unification formula. In the Formula for National Reconciliation and Democratic Unification, President Chun suggested that a constitution for a unified nation be drafted at a Consultative Conference for National Reunification formed with representatives of the two areas, which would then be adopted through free and democratic referendums held throughout the whole peninsula. The formula stipulates that the unification of the country can be accomplished by organizing a unified legislature and establishing a unified government through a general election held under the constitution of the unified Korea.

As a practical arrangement leading to unification, the formula also called for the conclusion of a Provisional Agreement on Basic Relations between South and North Korea. The gist of the suggested agreement was 1) maintenance of inter-Korean relations on the principle of reciprocity and equality, 2) peaceful solution of issues through dialogue, 3) recognition of each other's socio-political system and non-interference in internal affairs, 4) adherence to the existing Armistice Agreement and termination of the arms race, 5) opening of the two societies to each other, 6) respect for each other's international treaties, and 7) establishment of a resident liaison in Seoul and P'yŏngyang.

Announcing the formula, President Chun proposed a South-North preparatory meeting to arrange a conference between the top leaders of the two sides as he had suggested earlier, so that they could exchange opinions on the new formula.

The unification formula is especially significant in that it expressly sets forth principles for peaceful unification, that is, unification must be accomplished on the principle of national self-determination, and through democratic and peaceful procedures that reflect the free will of the entire 60 million people of South and North Korea.

Economy

The integrated steel mill of the Pohang Iron and Steel Co.

Rapid Transformation

Korea today is ranked as a newly industrializing country with a potential to join the ranks of the developed economies in the not so distant future. But at the beginning of the 1960s, the Republic of Korea had all the problems of a resource-poor, low-income developing country with the bulk of its population dependent on scarce farmland for bare subsistence.

Korea's per capita gross national product in 1961 stood at a meager US$82, near the bottom of the international income scale. Already densely populated, the country had an annual population growth of three percent adding to a serious unemployment and under-employment problem. Domestic savings and exports were both insignificant. In addition, Korea had not yet fully recovered from the devastation of the Korean War (1950-53).

During the two decades since, however, the Korean scene has been drastically transformed, almost beyond recognition. This has been due largely to the successful implementation of a series of five-year economic development plans launched in 1962. By 1984, the GNP in real terms increased to US$81 billion, with the real per capita GNP reaching US$1998. At the same time, exports rose nearly 550 times to US$29.2 billion last year, due basically to soaring foreign sales of an increasing variety of manufactured goods. Exports have thus been the leading edge of Korean economic progress.

The industrial sector—mining and manufacturing—grew at an annual average of about 13 percent between 1962 and 1984, nearly twice as fast as the economy as a whole. As a result, the industrial share of the GNP increased from 16 percent in 1962 to 32 percent in 1984. The agricultural sector, growing at a

116

slower four percent, declined from 37 percent of the GNP to 15 percent in the same period. The share of services rose slightly from 47 percent to 52.6 percent.

In keeping with rapid economic growth, employment nearly doubled from 7.7 million persons in 1963 to just over 14 million by 1984. The work force in 1984 broke down to 3.9 million in agriculture (including 0.18 million in fishing), 3.5 million in industry (0.14 million in mining plus 3.36 million in manufacturing) and 6.6 million in services. Agriculture accounted for 27.1 percent of total employment in 1984, industry for 24.2 percent and services for 48.7 percent. In comparison, the 1963 ratios were 63.1 percent agriculture, 8.7 percent industry and 28.2 percent services. The rate of unemployment decreased from 8.2 percent in 1963 to a low of 3.2 percent in 1978, then rising to 5.2 percent in 1980 and coming down again to 3.8 percent in 1984.

Foreign Trade

Because Korea is poorly endowed in natural resources, trade is its life line. Korea has thus been giving top priority to export expansion so that it can pay for raw materials and capital goods needed to sustain economic growth.

Exports rose from US$55 million in 1962 to US$29.2 billion in 1984 in terms of current market prices, recording a nominal average annual growth of 36.7 percent. In more recent years, however, the growth rate slowed to around 20 percent owing partly to worldwide recession and partly to the passing of the earlier period of rapid export increases from a very low

Composition of Export-Import Market (1984)

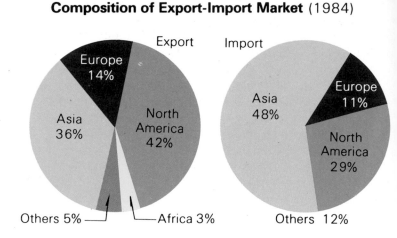

Export

Europe 14%

Asia 36%

North America 42%

Others 5% — — Africa 3%

Import

Asia 48%

Europe 11%

North America 29%

Others 12%

level. Exports in 1984 were 95 percent manufactured goods. Major export items were steel, non-ferrous metals, industrial machinery and plants, ships, automobiles, electronics, textiles, footwear, plywood, auto tires and plastic products.

Imports increased from US$422 million in 1962 to US$30.6 billion in 1984, growing at an average annual rate of 23.8 percent. Even though imports have been rising more slowly than exports, Korea has been experiencing a chronic trade gap, due at least in part to the high cost of imported energy. In 1984, oil accounted for 18.8 percent of the total imports, capital goods for 33.0 percent and grain, raw materials and other products for 48.2 percent.

Korea's trading partners have also been increasingly expanded and diversified. For instance, in 1962, the United States of America and Japan together took 57 percent of Korea's exports and supplied 79 percent of its imports. Their combined shares in 1984, however, were down to 51.5 percent of exports and 47.3 percent of imports. Korea today trades with virtually all countries in the world.

The country's trade gap has also been drastically reduced over the past two decades or so. In 1963, imports were 5.7 times larger than exports but in 1984, imports exceeded exports by only 5 percent. Trade deficits in earlier days were filled mainly with foreign aid. But lately, however, they have been covered with earnings from the export of services and foreign loans. Since Korea's debt service ratio is on a manageable level and its exports continue to rise, the country continues to enjoy good credit standing on the international financial market

Industrial Development

During the initial stages of Korean industrialization, labor-intensive light industry, especially textiles, was the growth leader but more recently, rapidly developing heavy and chemical industries have come to account for over half of the total manufacturing output. In 1984, Korea became the 10th largest steel producer in the world with the completion of the project to increase the annual production capacity of the Pohang Iron and Steel Company facility from 5.5 million metric tons to 9.10 million tons. This raised the nation's total steel-making capacity to 14.5 million tons a year. Steel exports in 1984 totaled US$2.66 billion. Furthermore the fast expanding shipbuilding industry in 1984 exported US$2.71 billion worth of vessels, up 50.7 percent over 1983.

The country is also developing the production of a

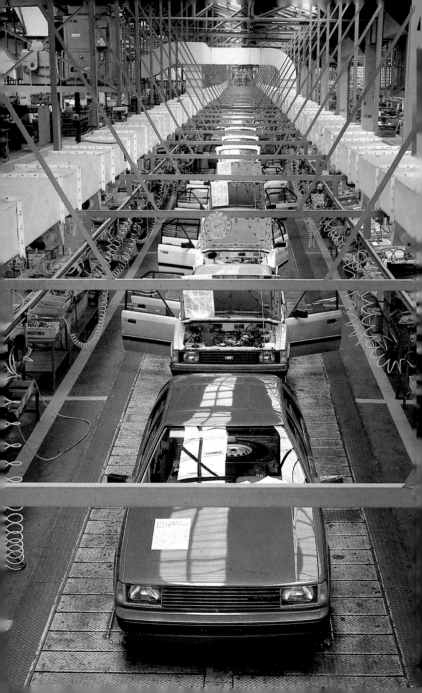

wide range of industrial machinery and equipment. At the heart of this effort is the huge machinery industrial complex at Ch'angwon, on the southern coast. Among the many modern facilities at Ch'angwon is the plant of the Korea Heavy Industries and Construction Company, dedicated in June 1982; the largest of its kind in Korea, this plant produces power plant equipment, construction machinery and industrial plants.

The electronics industry is also a major growth sector and an increasingly important foreign exchange earner as well. In 1984, the industry produced about US$7.17 billion worth of various products, about three-fifths of which were exported. Products now, include television sets, stereo equipment, tape recorders, radios, electronic watches, citizens band transceivers, TV games, calculators, video tape recorders, audio and video cassette tapes, microwave ovens, semiconductors and small computers.

In 1984, Korea manufactured 260,000 motor vehicles of various kinds including passenger cars, trucks and buses, registering a 24 percent increase over 1983. About 52,000 vehicles, chiefly small cars, were sold overseas in 1984.

Two large petrochemical complexes have been developed to help meet increasing domestic demands. Currently, the nation has a naphtha cracking capacity of 505,000 tons in ethylene equivalent and a downstream production capacity of 1.62 million tons of plastics, synthetic rubber and other synthetic materials. This industry is supported by several large oil

Automobile assembly plants are being built throughout the country as exports of Korean cars and trucks are on the rise.

refineries with a combined daily crude processing capacity of 792,000 barrels.

The textile industry, one of the oldest manufacturing businesses in Korea, is still a major exchange earner. Production in 1984 included 393 million square meters of cotton fabrics, 12 million square meters of pure worsted fabrics and 1,033 billion square meters of synthetic fiber fabrics. The industry has a chemical fiber production capacity of 1,645 tons per day.

Other principal industrial products of Korea include cement, processed foods, leather goods, plywood, paper and paper products, chemical fertilizers, agricultural pesticides, soap, automotive tires, footwear, ceramics, glass and glass products, nonferrous metals, power tillers and other farm implements, and sewing machines.

Overseas Construction

Korean construction firms operate in more than 30 foreign countries, with some 160,000 skilled Korean construction workers serving overseas. Overseas construction contracts have gained Koreans a considerable reputation throughout the world for their skill, perseverance, determination and diligence. Korean builders are now operating in the main in the Middle East, Southeast Asia, Africa and Latin America.

Low prices stemming from high-speed construction and cheap labor increase foreign demand for construction work.

Energy

Reflecting a rapid pace of industrialization, Korea's energy consumption has more than doubled over the past decade. Various forms of energy consumed in 1984 totaled the equivalent of 53.8 million metric tons of oil, compared to 20.9 million MT in 1971. Just over 75 percent of energy consumed in 1984 was imported, mostly in the form of crude oil and some in coal and nuclear fuel.

To lessen such a high dependence on oil imports, the nation is endeavoring to develop alternative sources of energy—principally nuclear power at present—while enforcing vigorous conservation measures. A long-term program is being implemented to drastically boost the share of nuclear power—which is now much cheaper than oil—in total electricity generated. The country has in fact decided recently not to build any more oil-fired power plants in the future.

The overall power-generating capacity of the country is scheduled to be increased from 14.2 million kilowatts in 1984 to 27 million kw in 1991, when the energy sources for power generation are projected to be 15 percent oil, 41 percent nuclear, 22 percent coal, 10 percent natural gas and 12 percent hydroelectric. In 1984, the comparable ratios were 49 percent oil, 22 percent nuclear, 25 percent coal and four percent hydroelectric, without any gas-fire power plant yet in existence. Electric power generated in 1984 totaled 53.8 billion kilowatt hours, compared with 11.5 billion kwh in 1971.

Thus far, the entire petroleum requirements of Korea have had to be imported as the country has yet to discover commercially feasible domestic oil reserves. Oil imports, mostly from the Middle East, increased from only one million MT in 1962 to 12 million MT (worth US$176 million) in 1972 and further to 28 million MT (valued at US$5.6 billion) in 1984.

The production of anthracite—the only type of coal mined in Korea and at the same time the principal household fuel—rose from 7.4 million MT in 1962 to just under 21 million MT in 1984. Due to limited deposits, however, anthracite mining can hardly be expanded much further and thus this fuel began to be imported in 1978 to keep pace with increasing demand. Anthracite imports rose from 646,000MT in 1978 to 804,000MT in 1984. To hold down demand for anthracite, a large percent of which is used in domestic heating and cooking, plans are being carried out to expand the supply of petroleum and natural gas for domestic fuel in cities.

Forest fuels—firewood and charcoal—accounted for over 50 percent of total energy consumption in Korea until as recently as 1962. But its share was down to a mere four percent in 1984.

The country is pushing ahead with projects to explore the continental shelf for oil and prospect and develop overseas oil, coal and uranium deposits in an effort to secure stable sources of energy resources.

Minerals

Apart from anthracite, Korea has sizable deposits of a large variety of metallic and nonmetallic minerals that are being commercially exploited. Mining, however, accounts for a mere one percent of the GNP.

Principal minerals mined in 1984 included 553.000

metric tons of iron ore, 4,480MT of tungsten concentrate, 52,000kg of refined silver, 212,000MT of kaolin, 31.2 million MT of limestone (mostly for cement), 20,000MT of lead ore and 106,000MT of zinc ore.

Mineral exports, including tungsten, talc, agalmatolite and graphite, totaled US$92 million in 1984, compared to US$83 million in 1978, while mineral imports, such as iron, zinc, copper and aluminum ores, approximated US$1 billion, double the 1978 level. Mineral imports are likely to outpace mineral exports even more rapidly in the future as Korea is self-sufficient in only a very limited variety. Korea is now in the process of developing mineral mining overseas to help supply increasing domestic needs.

Agriculture

Korea's overall agricultural production doubled between 1962 and 1976. Growth since then, however, has tended to slow down, but the much-emphasized goal of self-sufficiency in rice—the most important staple food crop—has once again been obtained.

Agricultural development efforts have been concentrated mainly on maximizing yield on the country's limited arable land—corresponding to only 22.2 percent of total land area, the bulk of which is mountainous. New high-yield varieties of rice and other crops have been introduced, together with better farming methods. Irrigation has been continually expanded by damming rivers and pumping up ground water. A large domestic fertilizer and pesticide industry has been developed to keep farmers adequately supplied with these products. Major proportions of rice paddies have been restructured for more efficient farming and to permit mechanization as well. Furthermore, the *Saemaŭl Undong* (New Community Movement), an integrated rural development program, was initiated at the beginning of the 1970s, resulting in enormous changes in the village scene. Through the movement, numerous village-level self-help projects have been carried out throughout the countryside to improve and expand housing, roads, water supply, drainage, communal facilities, irrigation and other rural infrastructure in conjunction with extensive rural electrification. Off-season local industries or workshops have also been established through the *Saemaŭl Undong* to further raise rural incomes.

In 1984, Korea produced, from two million hectares of land, just under 7.3 million metric tons of food grains, including 5.6 million MT of rice, 804,000MT of barley, 254,000MT of soybeans and 133,000MT of corn (maize). The 1962 grain production totaled only five million tons.

There has been a rapid growth in fruits, vegetables and other high-value cash crops, and livestock products, the demand for which has been increasing rapidly in tune with the rising income standards of the people. For example, the production of apples leaped from 118,000MT in 1962 to 528,000 in 1984; tangerines from 800MT to 261,000; grapes from 8,000MT to 125,000; pears from 27,000MT to 101,000; and peaches from 20,000MT to 98,000, while persimmons went from 27,000MT to 69,000. The rapid spread of plastic green houses has been a major factor in the increased size of the vegetable harvest which has helped the average farm household to catch up with the average urban working family in annual income in the mid-1970s and maintain this equilibrium until today.

Through infrastructure expansion and cultivation of

high-yield hybrid seeds, Korea has boosted rice production.

Recent efforts to increase agricultural production were focused on boosting the rate of self-sufficiency in rice, which stood at 88 percent in 1980 but rose to just over 100 percent by 1985. Under this policy, further farm mechanization, particularly the large-scale introduction of rice transplanting and harvesting machines, is being pushed in order to solve the problem of increasingly acute rural labor shortages during the seasons of peak agricultural activity. This problem has been created by increasing migration to urban-industrial centers. The farm population, which remained virtually static at a little over 15 million until 1969, decreased to just under nine million in 1984. The proportion of rural population in the national population dropped from 57 percent in 1962 to only 22.2 percent by 1984. (The average arable land holding per farm household, however, has remained little changed at around only one hectare since the mid-1970s.)

In fact, farm mechanization has been vigorously pursued since the early 1970s. Between 1970 and 1984, the number of power tillers in use jumped from 12,000 to 538,000; power pumps for irrigation from 54,000 to 273,000; power sprayers and dusters from 45,000 to 473,000; and power threshing machines from 41,000 to 287,000. Rice transplanting and harvesting machines have been distributed in growing numbers.

Irrigation facilities are being expanded further with the goal of raising the proportion of irrigated paddy land from 69 percent in 1980 to 76 percent by 1986. A search for even higher-yield rice and other crops is vigorously continuing, together with price support for major grains and free technical services to farmers.

Increased production and consumption of barley is being promoted as an effective way to conserve rice, in light of the fact that barley can be produced during winter as a second crop on rice fields which would otherwise lie idle. Due to the difficulty of adequately feeding 40 million people with the domestic harvest alone, it is likely that Korea will have to continue to import large quantities of wheat, and soybeans, as well as corn (mostly for animal feed), even after permanent rice self-sufficiency is achieved.

The production of livestock and livestock products increased drastically between 1962 and 1984. On farms at the end of 1984 were 2.3 million head of native draft cattle, 334,400 head of dairy cattle, 3 million pigs, 46.5 million chickens, 385,000 goats and 511,000 rabbits. Sericulture, an important source of farm income and export earnings, has declined in recent years owing to adverse developments in the international silk markets. Silk cocoon output decreased from a peak of 41,700MT in 1976 to only 9,500MT in 1984.

Forestry

An intensified nationwide reforestation movement has been in force since the early 1970s to green the once largely denuded forestlands, totalling 6.5 million hectares, or 67 percent of the total land area of the country. Forest timber thus increased from only 70 million cubic meters in 1970 to 164.4 million cubic meters in 1984 and continues to grow. Korea is now widely regarded as a model for reforestation in the developing world.

Vigorous measures are being taken to annually plant numerous trees, nurse newly planted ones and protect

The morning ebb tide. Laver screens

rise above the glittering surface.

old ones, while developing new varieties that are more productive and more resistant to pests and disease. To conserve forest resources until they become fully productive, tree cutting is strictly controlled. For over a decade, timber production has been held to around one million cubic meters and the annual production of firewood and charcoal has been limited to less than five million tons. These efforts have greatly contributed to flood and soil erosion control as well.

Fisheries

Major efforts have been made over the past two decades to expand and modernize Korea's fishing industry, an important source not only of protein food but also foreign exchange earnings. Fish catches increased from 470,000 metric tons in 1962 to over 2.9 million MT in 1984, while fishery exports jumped from US$12.3 million to US$1 billion. During the same period, the nation's fishing-vessel tonnage rose from 161,000 gross tons to 828,000GT. The number of vessels increased much more slowly, going from 45,000 to 88,600 during the period under review, reflecting the fact that larger, motorized vessels have replaced numerous small sail or row boats under a fishing fleet modernization program.

A particularly rapid growth was registered by deep-sea fishing. Deep-sea catches from the seven seas by the Korean fishing fleet leaped from a mere 657MT in 1962 to a peak of 724,000MT in 1976. The volume then fell to 458,000MT in 1980, though it recovered partially to 658,000MT in 1984. The setback is attributable to rising fuel prices, the declaration by many nations of 200-mile economic sea zones and a global economic recession. Korea has negotiated fisheries agreements with a number of coastal nations to secure fishing rights in their economic waters and is continuing efforts to prop up the deep-sea fishing industry.

The growth of offshore fishing has also slowed down in recent years, owing basically to limited marine resources in the waters around Korea. Offshore catches totaled 1.5 million MT in 1984, up only slightly from 1.25 million MT in 1976. To take up the slack, intensive efforts are being made to develop coastal aquaculture, which produced 680,000MT in 1984, nearly two times the output 10 years before.

Investment

Sharp rises in investment and domestic saving have fueled the high growth of the Korean economy in the past two decades. The ratio of investment to the GNP rose from only 13.2 percent in 1961 to 22 percent by 1967 and further to 31 percent in 1974, remaining steadily on similarly high levels ever since. Especially since the middle 1970s, intensive investment has been made in the development of heavy and chemical industries to accelerate Korean industrialization.

Up until the early 1960s, investments for economic development had to be financed mainly with foreign savings—mostly in the form of net increases in overseas borrowing—as domestic savings were low. The ratio of domestic savings to the GNP, however, soon began to climb upward rapidly in tune with rising income standards of the nation, going from less than five percent in 1961 to 13 percent by 1967 and leaping to 22 percent in 1973. During the 1977-81 period, the domestic savings ratio averaged 24.4 percent, covering about three-fourths of the total investment requirements. Efforts are being made to increase the domestic savings ratio to over 27 percent on the average during the fifth plan period (1982-86) to help achieve an annual GNP growth rate of seven to eight percent, even with a further reduction in the foreign savings ratio.

In absolute terms, inflows of foreign capital—medium and long-term loans and equity investments—have continued to expand since the early 1960s, making important contributions to economic growth. Capital inflows totaled only US$300 million during the first plan (1962-66) but jumped to US$10.7 billion during the fourth plan (1977-81). The fifth plan (1982-86) is projected to require a capital inflow of US$35 billion, which should not be overly difficult to obtain in view of Korea's high international credit standing owing to its past remarkable economic success.

In the coming years, the country will emphasize for-

Investment and Finance

In billion *Won*

	1981	1982	1983	1984
Gross Investment	13,342.9	13,979.8	16,225.3	19,591.9
(Percent of GNP)	(24.1)	(27.0)	(27.8)	(30.0)
Domestic Savings	9,918.7	11,593.9	14,515.8	17,931.0
(Percent of GNP)	(21.7)	(22.4)	(24.8)	(27.4)
Foreign Savings	3,506.5	2,319.5	1,679.4	1,510.6
(Percent of GNP)	(7.7)	(4.5)	(2.9)	(2.3)
Statistical Discrepancy	-82.2	66.3	30.0	150.2
(Percent of GNP)	(-0.2)	(0.1)	(0.1)	(0.2)

Source: Major Statistics of Korean Economy 1985

eign direct investment even more vigorously than in the past, especially to facilitate the transfer of advanced technologies and managerial expertise—key elements in improving Korean competitiveness abroad. A comprehensive range of tax holidays and reduced taxes are provided to new companies with foreign capital. As a general rule, joint venture with domestic partners, with foreign equity limited to 50 percent, are being promoted. But this and other restrictions on foreign investment are slated to be progressively eased in keeping with the country's open-door economic policy. Already, most types of industry have been opened up for foreign investment.

Science and Technology

Korea is striving to whittle down its technology gap with developed countries as the key to becoming an advanced industrial nation during the 1980s. A five-year science and technology promotion program was launched in 1982 with the aim of boosting the country's investments in research and development from only 0.7 percent of the gross national product in 1979 to two percent by 1986, only slightly lower than the average currently obtained in industrial countries. In monetary terms, the projected 1986 investments translate into US$3.2 billion, compared with only US$600 million realized in 1979.

At the same time, a quarterly Technology Promotion Conference, presided over by the President, was instituted to discuss and plan effective steps to ensure the success of the program. The conference is participated in by high-level representatives of the government,

The Hanil Synthetic Fiber Industrial Co. in Masan produces

synthetic fiber for export as well as domestic use.

research institutions and the academic and business communities.

In 1981, 15 government-supported research institutions were merged into nine and placed under the sole administrative jurisdiction of the Ministry of Science and Technology for more efficient and effective coordination of their activities. These institutes are being provided with larger resources to spearhead the nation's drive for technological advancement. The reorganization included the merger of the Korea Institute of Science and Technology (KIST), a multidisciplinary contract research organization founded in 1966, and the Korea Advanced Institute of Science, an independent graduate school established in 1970, into the Korea Advanced Institute of Science and Technology (KAIST). With the integration of R & D activities and academic programs, KAIST will play an even more important role in the advancement of scientific knowledge and technological expertise in Korea.

In addition, a research complex is being developed in Taedŏk County near the provincial capital of Taejŏn, some 150 kilometers south of Seoul, in order to increase economic efficiency in research by promoting joint use of facilities, personnel and information. The "Taedŏk Science Town," covering an area of 28 square kilometers, now contains 10 research institutes and three universities. It will have a total of 30 R & D institutions by 1990 when the town is completed.

The fields of research currently assigned top government priorities include semiconductors, computers, mechanical engineering and automation, fine chemistry, telecommunications, safety in nuclear power plants and pollution control.

Tax incentives and other public assistance are provided to encourage the establishment and expansion of R & D personnel and facilities. The number of R & D institutes increased from 105 in 1965 to 1,157 in 1983, comprising 156 supported by the government, public agencies and non-profit organizations, 278 at colleges and universities and 723 operated by private firms. The number of researchers employed jumped from only 2,800 to nearly 30,309 in the same period, while total R & D expenditures leaped fom a paltry two billion *won* to 621.7 billion *won* including 451 billion spent by private industries.

To further accelerate R & D activities in the private sector, the Korea Technology Development Corporation (KTDC) was founded in 1981 with a total initial asset valued at US$100 million, contributed by the government, industry and the World Bank. KTDC provides long-term low interest loans and equity capital to industry to help finance R & D activities, the early commercialization of R & D results and the introduction of advanced technologies from abroad. Two similar private firms are being set up.

The government is taking various measures to facilitate technical transfers from overseas, including reductions in official red tape involved in foreign technology licensing, the conclusion of technical cooperation agreements with foreign governments and international organizations, and the encouragement of foreign direct investments incorporating advanced technical know-how.

To meet the rapidly expanding demand for scientific and technical manpower, a major emphasis is placed on the training of scientists, engineers, craftsmen and other skilled workers at universities, junior colleges, vocational schools and so forth. An official projection shows that Korea's technical manpower should increase from 736,000 persons in 1981 to over 1.4 million in 1991. An increasing number of scientists and engineers are being sent abroad for advanced

Workers at The Korea Micro Electronic Co.

assemble semi-conductors for export.

training, while expatriate scientists and engineers are encouraged to return home to contribute their talents and skills to domestic technological advancement. Science education at preschool, elementary and secondary levels is also being vigorously promoted.

The Korea Science and Technology Information Center (KORSTIC) was merged in 1981 with the International Economic Research Institute into the Korea Institute for Industrial Economics and Technology to provide up-to-date and detailed information on overseas industrial and technological developments to Korean industry so that it can compete more effectively in world markets.

Korea is thus racing to meet the high technology challenges of the coming decades to sustain economic growth, especially by continuing to boost the exports of more sophisticated and better-quality products produced with greater efficiency.

Future Prospects

In view of its past economic performance and future growth potential, Korea is expected to maintain an annual economic growth rate of 7-8 percent well into the 21st century. Its gross national product should thus rise from about US$81 billion in 1984 to over US$250 billion (at 1984 prices) by the year 2000. With the population projected to increase from 40 million to nearly 50 million in the meantime, per capita GNP is expected to increase from US$2,000 to US$5,000. By 2000, Korea is predicted to emerge as the 15th largest economy and the 10th largest trading nation in the world.

A steel worker.

A scientist uses an electron microscope to unravel cryptic DNA spirals at a major genetic engineering research center in the Taedŏk Science Town, Ch'ungch'ŏngnam-do Province.

Projections for the Korean Economy through 2000

	Unit	1984	1990	2000	Average annual growth rate, %	
					1985-90	1991-2000
Population	Million	40.6	44.1	49.4	1.38	1.14
GNP	Trillion *won*, current prices	65.3	119.2	342.3	10.7	12.3
	Trillion *won*, 1980 prices	49.1	75.8	147.1	7.5	6.8
	(US$ billion, 1984 prices)	(81.1)	(125.6)	(252.0)	7.8	7.2
Per capita GNP	Thousand *won*, current prices	1,595	2,693	6,837	9.1	9.8
	Thousand *won*, 1980 prices	1,211	1,719	2,978	6.0	6.0
	(US$, 1984 prices)	(1,998)	(2,849)	(5,103)	6.2	6.0
GNP deflator	1980=100	131.6	157.2	232.7	3.0	4.0
Merchandise exports	US$ billion, current prices	29.2	62.46	230.92	15.3	14.0
Merchandise imports	US$ billion, current prices	30.6	61.49	223.97	14.2	13.8
Gross foreign debt	US$ billion	44.1	62.5[1]	54.0		
Housing owner-ship	%	67.0	68.8	82.2		
Hours worked	Per week	54[2]	45.0	41.0		
Average life span	Years	66[2]		72		

[1] For 1984
[2] For 1980

Source: Korea Development Institute

Exports are projected to rise from about US$29 billion in 1984 to US$230 billion (at current prices) in 2000, while imports should increase from US$30 billion to US$224 billion. The country's current account is expected to begin to consistently register a surplus toward the end of the 1980s. By the end of the 1990s, Korea should become a net capital exporting country capable of providing substantial levels of official development assistance, as well as technical aid and import credits, to less developed countries.

Much of Korea's future growth should come from the development of more sophisticated industries, such as automobiles, machinery, electronics and fine chemicals. The share of industry in the GNP should rise from 29.4 percent in 1983 to over 33 percent by 2000, while that of agriculture should decline from 14.2 percent to 8.3 percent. Meantime, the share of services should increase from 53.5 percent to nearly 59 percent. Korea is thus expected to attain an economic structure similar to those now commonly found in developed countries.

Koreans are thus expected to become much more affluent by the beginning of the next century. The number of cars per 100 people is projected to increase to over 26, from just under one in 1983, while the number of telephones per 100 people should rise from 12 to 39. The percentage of families owning refrigerators should increase from 38 to over 90. There should also be remarkable improvements in housing, roads, school facilities and other infrastructure.

The average working hours per week should decrease from 54 to 41, giving a powerful stimulus to the growth of leisure and sports industries. The average life span of Koreans is expected to increase from 66 to 72.

Saemaŭl Undong

Newly built Saemaŭl houses mirrored on a nearby river.

Birth of a National Movement

Since the *Saemaŭl Undong* (New Community Movement), devised and introduced by President Park Chung Hee, came into operation in 1971, it has become a nationwide movement training rural and, more recently, urban people in the benefits of diligence, self-help and cooperation, encouraging the balanced growth of industry and agriculture, and promoting national integrity. In a word, the *Saemaŭl Undong* is a national movement designed to enable the Korean people to banish the dark legacy of the nation's past and to bring about national modernization and development through integrated endeavors encouraged not by theories and ideals but by action and practice.

Saemaŭl Undong has proved unique in terms of its impact on the modernization of a developing country. No program of other developing countries has mobilized so much social, administrative and popular support, or brought about such a dramatic impact on rural development and national integrity as the *Saemaŭl Undong* of Korea. Here lies the reason why the *Saemaŭl* Movement is drawing increasing attention from the international community concerned with rural enlightenment in developing countries. This interest is demonstrated by the fact that a total of 26,491 foreigners from 118 countries (as of May 31, 1985) have visited Korea to learn about the developmental process of *Saemaŭl Undong*.

Indigenous to Korea

Saemaŭl Undong is characterized by two basic features which may be unfamiliar to foreigners. First, unlike integrated rural development programs about which many theories have been propounded and many pilot schemes adopted, the *Saemaŭl* Movement started without a well-defined formal or theoretical framework. Only recently have efforts to theorize about the *Saemaŭl* Movement started after much practical progress has been made. Second, the *Saemaŭl* Movement is a purely Korean concept, so the slogans and terminology used are of purely Korean origin.

Saemaŭl Undong originated in the unfavorable side-effects brought about in the agricultural sector by the miraculous economic growth of the first and second five-year economic development plans (1962-1966 and 1967-1971) which emphasized industrial development and expansion of export capacity. The successful implementation of the two five-year plans resulted in an 85 percent increase in gross national product in 10 years and an increase in national per capita income from $95 in 1961 to $252 in 1971. Growth in the agricultural sector, however, lagged far behind that in the industrial sector as the government could not pay equal attention to agriculture. The average rate of growth per annum during the first five-year plan period (1962-1966) was 7.8 percent, but agriculture grew only 5.3 percent per annum during the period. The situation grew worse during the second five-year plan (1967-1971), when the agricultural sector grew only 2.5 percent per annum while average growth of total industry was 10.5 percent.

As a result of the successful implementation of the two five-year plans, the gap between the annual incomes of farm households and urban dwellers grew wider. On the average, a farm household earned 71 percent of that of an urban wage earner's household in 1962, and the figure fell to 61 percent in 1970, when farmers with less than one hectare of land, constituting about 67 percent of Korean farmers, earned only 50 percent of the income of urban wage earners.

The deteriorating rural situation widened the gap between factory and farm, and became a major cause for a rapid migration of the rural population into large cities. In the 1950s the farming population constituted about 70 percent of the total population, but the figure decreased to 46 percent in 1971. Such tremendous population pressure on urban areas exacerbated many typical urban problems.

Besides, many difficulties such as serious labor shortages occurred in rural areas, where mechanization was not yet known, because of negative attitudes among farmers. The quality of labor also deteriorated because mostly the aged and women remained in rural areas, so most villages were left without potential lead-

Vinyl hothouses have increased farm incomes immensely and

ers since those who moved away were the relatively well educated young men.

Balanced Growth

Aware of this situation, the government policy for the Third Five-Year Economic Development Plan (1972-1976) emphasized "balanced growth between industry and agriculture" and development of agriculture and fisheries especially, as the first of the three basic objectives for the third plan. (The other two objectives were increased exports and construction of

have made fresh fruits and vegetables available year round.

Restaurant employees
sweep streets and tend
flowers planted in pots
along the sidewalk as
part of the urban
Saemaŭl Movement.
Building roads, planting
trees and other
enviromental programs
have given a face-lift to
rural Korea.

heavy industry.) During the period, the government planned to invest nearly $2 billion in agricultural development. As monetary investment alone is not sufficient for agricultural development, the agricultural sector, especially the farmers, had to be ready to make effective use of such investment in order to maximize efficiency.

Without fostering confidence among the farmers in a bright and positive future, the government's efforts for agricultural development would have been less effective. People must have a positive attitude toward development and feel confident that "We too can prosper if we work hard and cooperate with each other." In this sense, some sort of nationwide mass movement strongly supported by political power and the administrative machinery became necessary to cultivate positive attitudes in the rural masses, to assist them in gaining confidence in their future, and to train them for more active self-reliance and cooperation. Thus basic directions for the *Saemaŭl Undong* were given and experimental projects started in rural villages in 1971.

General Guiding Principles

A step-by-step approach was considered necessary for the success of *Saemaŭl Undong*. The early projects were designed to improve the living conditions of individual families. Roofs were repaired and kitchens and toilets improved, with the government supplying materials and advice and the farmer doing the work. This was to instill the spirit of self-help. During the next stage, the villagers were encouraged to meet together, choose a *Saemaŭl* leader, and carry out projects which would improve the village environment and contribute to the improvement of farm life. The building of bridges, roads, irrigation and water facilities, common laundry places, common compost plots and village halls were typical of projects during this stage. These projects gave the villagers experience in organization and cooperation. In the third stage, villagers were encouraged to take up projects which would increase individual income. Group farming, common seed beds, vegetable cultivation, pig, chicken and cattle farming, community forestation, *Saemaŭl* factories and common marketing facilities were some of the projects chosen at this stage. The projections into the immediate future include plans to build and extend health and sanitation projects and to shift from village projects to intervillage projects.

As *Saemaŭl Undong* is a nationwide movement strongly supported by the government, basic guidelines for the preparation of projects are issued by a Central Consultative Council which is chaired by the Minister of Home Affairs. Based on these guidelines, a village project is selected by the village Development Committee, subject to the approval of the General Assembly of the village. The project selected is coordinated with other projects by the *myŏn* (township) chief in consultation with the *myŏn Saemaŭl Undong* Committee. The coordinated projects are reported to the county chief who approves the projects in coordination with the county *Saemaŭl* Consultative Council. Only projects in dispute are referred to the Provincial Governor, who solves the problem in a similar way in consultation with the provincial *Saemaŭl* Consultative Council. In such a way, all the projects are finally summarized and coordinated at the *Saemaŭl* Central Consultative Council, chaired by the Minister of Home

Affairs.

At the non-governmental level, the Movement is coordinated by the Central Office of *Saemaŭl Undong,* which represents all non-governmental *Saemaŭl* organizations. These include among others the Central *Saemaŭl* Leaders Association, the Central Federation of *Saemaŭl* Women's Clubs, the Factory *Saemaŭl Undong* Headquarters and the Central Council of Business-and-Office *Saemaŭl Undong.*

Leadership Training

For effective implementation of the *Saemaŭl* Movement, leadership training and villagers' participation have received special emphasis. Leadership training is conducted through two programs, a village *Saemaŭl* leaders training program and a social leaders training program, both of which aim at enlightening the people. For any *Saemaŭl* project, voluntary and active participation of the villagers is the basic requirement. Thus, participation is required of all villagers—regardless of level of education and standard of living—in planning, selecting, financing, implementing and maintaining a project.

Perhaps the most important achievement of *Saemaŭl Undong* is its impact on the morale of the people. It has had a definite impact on promoting a cooperative spirit at the grassroots level, which is the basis for any rural development activity, and on giving the people faith in a bright and positive future. The pessimistic attitude which prevailed before 1970 has gradually changed and people have begun to look forward to a brighter future. At the same time, confidence among

the people ("We too can prosper" and "We can do it")
has been developed. Of the 2,000 farmers sampled in
1975, about a half expressed the belief that they
expected to be able to enjoy as high a living standard
as city people by 1980, while only 10 percent of the
farmers had a negative opinion.

Urban Participation

As is well known, the Korean economy continued to
grow with surprising speed. Particularly the agricultural sector made astonishing progress under the
Saemaŭl Undong. This was basically due to the promotion of the *Saemaŭl* spirit.

In Korea, the *Saemaŭl Undong* is used as a training
vehicle to enable people to solve their own problems.
After twelve years of the Movement, the initiative was
gradually turned over to the people, and more and
more villages began participating in the process, which
requires a greater cooperative spirit. Especially the
urban *Saemaŭl* Movement, initiated in 1974, empha-
sizing the basic philosophy that no citizen should be
excluded from a popular movement designed to bring
about common prosperity, has contributed to arming
urban societies with a cooperative attitude, strong ethical sense, and sound management of community life
through such activities as maintaining order in urban
life, helping less privileged neighbors, cleaning up the
city, fostering friendship with neighbors, helping the
rural *Saemaŭl* Movement, etc. *Saemaŭl Undong* has
placed particular emphasis on actual practice rather
than words. It has tried to teach that completion of the
simplest task is worth much more than eloquent
speeches or tons of paperwork.

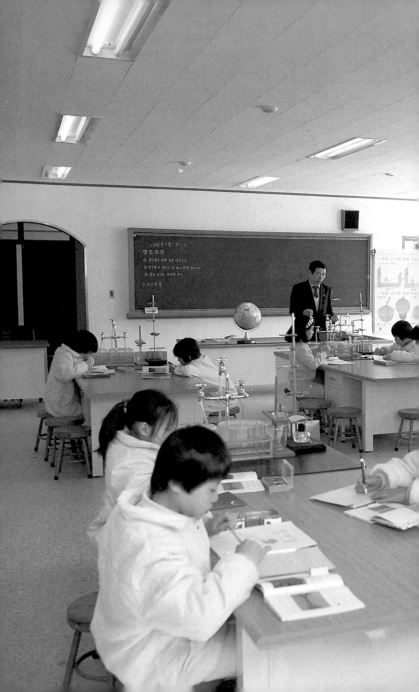

Education

Children study science in a modern, well-equipped laboratory.

It was not until 1885 that Korea's first modern school was built, and even then the internal political chaos followed by colonization of Korea by Japan delayed modern universal education until after World War II. The development of education was again interrupted by the Korean War in the 1950s when all schools had to take refuge in the southern part of Korea, and most students took up arms to defend the country. After the Armistice in 1953, educational facilities were again developed with great determination. The Confucian doctrine that saw education as the key to future success was deeply ingrained in the Korean mind; after 1953, both popular demand and concerted government effort led to impressive growth.

The foundation of Korean education is a democratic philosophy that guarantees equal opportunity for education and respect for individual ability. Besides providing basic knowledge, the purpose of Korean education is to instill within the student those values and skills necessary for the regeneration of the nation. Within a few short years, Korea has risen from poverty to industrialization, with an accompanying complexity of social life. It is the goal of education not only to assist students to take a creative part in a new society, but to teach them the ability to make judgements consistent with the traditional Korean value system of filial piety and loyalty to the nation.

Koreans are a history-conscious people. Korean history and culture are constantly being studied and reevaluated in light of the renaissance now taking place within society. It is thus also the aim of Korean education to promote a historical consciousness in students that generates pride in the nation and an awareness of the rich Korean contribution to world culture.

While in the past education in Korea meant a liberal education, today the pressing needs of a new society have created an awareness of the dignity of manual labor and of the responsibility of education to assist in the acceleration of industrial growth. This is reflected in the government policy to encourage and promote technical and vocational education. Thus in recent years many technical and vocational high schools have been founded—many by large industries—while colleges and universities have been required to offer practical programs. Those in farming areas must provide departments of agriculture and those on the coast, departments of fisheries and oceanography, etc. There is no doubt that Korea's great progress in recent years can largely be attributed to the importance that Koreans have placed on education—both liberal and practical.

The Ministry of Education is responsible for the conduct of formal education, the compilation and copyright of texbooks and the maintenance of educational facilities. Special cities and provinces have boards of education which function as representative bodies. Under the boards are educational commissioners for each county and city, responsible for primary, middle and high school educational activities. The government advises these commissioners on basic educational matters and provides financial support.

Korea has adopted a school system dividing education into six-year elementary schools, three-year middle schools, three-year high schools and four-year colleges or universitites, with graduate school leading to a PhD degree. Two-year junior colleges and vocational colleges have also been established. There are now over 11.3 million children and young adults attending schools, colleges and universities in Korea. The number of teachers in these schools and colleges totaled 299,563 as of the end of 1984.

Education is continually under review and reforms

Number of Schools and Students

(As of 1984)

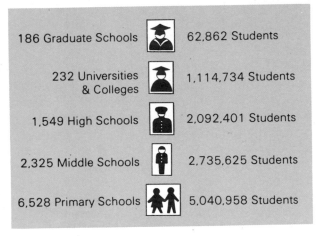

186 Graduate Schools		62,862 Students
232 Universities & Colleges		1,114,734 Students
1,549 High Schools		2,092,401 Students
2,325 Middle Schools		2,735,625 Students
6,528 Primary Schools		5,040,958 Students

are frequently made. In the recent past, the entrance examinations for middle and high school were abolished in preparation for the time when free compulsory education will be extended through middle school and to relieve the considerable pressure on middle school students to prepare for the exams, which resulted in a great financial burden to pay for outside tutors and an emotional burden for students. Secondary school textbooks have recently been revised. Other recent reforms include the enlarging of the quota for freshmen and the institution of night classes to enable young people who work to continue their education. Vocational education and vocational counseling at high schools have been strengthened so that students will be aware of the opportunities for work after high school and will be better able to judge their own capabilities. The government will take measures to increase enrollment at provincial colleges and universities and reduce the percentage of students migrating to Seoul to study.

For constant reform and development of the nation's educational programs, several specialized educational research institutes have been established. They include the National Institute of Education, responsible for developing educational theories in the socio-cultural context of Korea; the Korean Educational Development Institute, responsible for planning and implementing educational reform; provincial and county institutes, which research subjects of local concern; and many other private and public institutes. In 1985 the Council for Educational Reform was set up to report directly to the nation's chief executive. Composed of the nation's leading educators and school administrators as well as leaders from various walks of life, the council will work out an educational system best suited to Korea's present and future needs.

Elementary Education

As of 1984 there were 5,183 kindergartens, public and private, and 2,408 *Saemaŭl* children's institutes across the country. In a five-year plan starting in 1982, the number is set to be nearly doubled with an emphasis on the care of rural children through *Saemaŭl* institutes.

Six-year primary school in **Korea** is free and compulsory. As of the end of 1984, 5,040,958 children, or 98.3 percent of the school age population, attended elementary school. There were 6,528 schools with 1,020 branches staffed by 126,233 teachers. Graduates of elementary schools in 1984 totaled 924,452, of whom, 98.8 percent entered middle school.

Middle School

The number of primary school students entering middle school has increased significantly in recent years, due largely to improvements in the standard of living. Middle school (7th-9th grades) was made free and compulsory in remote areas and offshore islands in 1985 and will soon be made free and compulsory across the nation.

At the end of 1984, there were 2,325 middle schools with 2,735,625 students, 44 branches, and 66,372 teachers, Of the 741,494 graduates of middle school, 89.7 percent entered high school.

High School

High school is aimed at giving advanced liberal and technical education on the basis of what was achieved in middle school. In 1984 there were 1,549 high schools with 2,092,401 students and 66,278 teachers. Of these, 905 are general and 644 vocational. Vocational high schools have a total enrollment of 891,953.

The general high school offers required courses, electives and extracurricular activities. The Korean language, social studies, ethics and morality, Korean history, world history, geography, mathematics, biology, physical education, music and arts, English, and

Worker-students perform an experiment in dyeing. At the Hanil Industrial Girls High School, students are required to earn 204 academic credits during the three-year course.

management are required in all general high schools. However, different elective courses are offered in consideration of the future specialization of students in liberal arts or natural sciences.

The government has been placing greater emphasis on vocational and technical education to back up the sweeping industrialization programs of the country. Along this line, student quotas have been increased and new curricula added for engineering colleges, while a number of new vocational high schools have been established across the country. In addition, industries have been encouraged to establish and operate their own vocational training centers. The curriculum of vocational high schools is divided into general and professional courses which in turn consist of required and elective courses.

Educational System

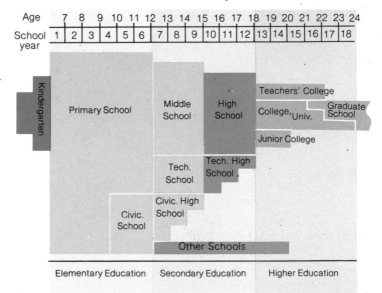

Higher Education

Higher education in Korea intends to instill in students an understanding of man and his environment, a desire to contribute to society, and a determination to improve the quality of life.

The number of students in each college and university in Korea is regulated by the government. In 1984 there were 870,170 students attending 99 four-year colleges and universities, including the largest women's university in the world; 62,862 in 186 graduate schools; 14,282 in 11 four-year teachers colleges; and 230,282 at 122 two-year junior colleges and miscellaneous vocational colleges across the country. The number of faculty members totaled 31,824. There also is a Radio Correspondence College offering 2 five-year college courses largely to working youths.

The government, in adjusting the ceiling of students to be enrolled in colleges and universities, puts importance on departments which are considered in higher demand by society. These include law, engineering, medicine, electronics and aeronautics. Colleges and universities recruit freshmen based on the results of a state-managed examination and on high school records.

Non-formal Education

About 98.3 percent of school-age children now attend primary school. In addition, the government is providing a wide range of non-formal educational programs, with the belief that learning should not stop with school. One form of non-formal education is the community education movement in which rural people are organized into classes, such as youth classes, women's classes, etc. These classes conduct their sessions in the evening. Local school buildings and facilities are available for their use after school hours. As part of the life-long education programs, a channel of KBS-TV is being used exclusively for educational purposes. In addition, Education Television (ETV) and Instructional Radio are operated by the Korean Educational Development Institute.

Scholarships and Grants

The government grants scholarships to deserving students so that they need not worry about continuing their study. Hitherto, financial aid available to students consisted of government loans, scholarships provided by private individuals, and exemptions from or reductions of tuition. To centralize these varied forms of scholarship for effective operation and award, a scholarship foundation was created by the government. The funds available for scholarships as well as the number of recipients also increased.

Overseas students who have special interest in Korean studies are encouraged to study in Korea under government scholarship grants. At the end of 1984 there were some 855 foreign students enrolled in Korea's colleges and universities.

Students who arrive here under government scholarships are free to choose which school to attend, and are aided by government officials in lodging and other incidental matters. They usually receive a year's language training prior to taking up their major studies,

Carrying on and extending the tradition of scholarship, education provides not only understanding of the arts and humanities but vocational skills as well.

which include such fields as economic and political development, the arts, language, medicine and the history of Korea.

Summer camp helps children develop their minds and bodies to meet the challenge of the future.

Public Libraries

Libraries play an important role in life-long education. There are three principal types of libraries; public, school and special. Public libraries must meet the informational needs of the public and stimulate the cultural development of the communities they serve. Many public libraries receive financial support from both the central government and the special city or provincial administrations and are also subject to their direction and supervision. School libraries are encouraged to be open to the public when practicable, and thus function as an important link with the community. There are also numerous private libraries, reading circles and circulating libraries in the 35,000 rural villages and cities throughout the country, helping to enhance the cultural standards of the populace.

Libraries

(As of 1984)

Classification	Number	Capacity (Person)	Size of Collection	Annual Users
National Library	1	2,069	972,583	887,143
National Assembly Library	1	246	612,001	49,465
Public Libraries	142	65,059	2,657,401	17,163,774
University Libraries	252	167,982	16,571,985	48,697,596
School Libraries	5,374	415,938	18,295,919	50,193,811
Special Libraries	229	7,295	3,565,428	1,417,480
Total	6,116	658,680	42,679,317	118,409,242

The 428km Seoul-Pusan Expressway.

Communications
and Transportation

Newspapers and Other Periodicals

There were several instances in Korean history, one as far back as 1577, when a sort of newspaper, *Chobo*, covering the activities of the court and government was put out in the capital. These ventures were never successful for more than a few issues until, in 1883, the thrice-monthly *Hansŏng Sunbo*, a government gazette that was required reading for all high officials, began to be published. A resurgence of conservatism the next year resulted in the destruction of the newspaper office by mobs and suspension of the publication.

But in 1886 a weekly paper printed in mixed Chinese and Korean type, called *Hansŏng Chubo*, succeeded it. This, however, ran for only two years before reactionary opinion resulted in its closing.

It was 10 years later, in 1896, that the first modern, privately-run, independent paper was established. The *Independent*, or *Tongnip Shinmun*, was run by Sŏ Chae-pil (Philip Jaisohn), a Korean medical doctor and independence leader educated in the United States. The paper was a crusading, progressive organ, printed partly in English and partly in the Korean phonetic alphabet, *han-gŭl*. It appeared every other day.

The most important of the pre-annexation papers was the *Taehan Maeil Shinbo*, which enjoyed comparative freedom to criticize the Japanese because its publisher, Ernest T. Bethel, was a British national. From its establishment in 1904, this paper was constantly subject to covert persecution by the authorities, however, and Bethel's untimely death around the time of annexation facilitated the eventual takeover of the paper as a mouthpiece for the Japanese authorities.

After a decade of suppression, Korean journalism experienced a limited revival in the early 1920s as part

Some of the national daily newspapers published in Seoul.

of the temporary liberalization of Japanese policy following the 1919 uprising (See History).

Three newspapers—*Dong-A Ilbo, Chosun Ilbo* and *Shisa Shinmun*—were permitted to publish under heavy censorship. During the 20 years before all papers were suppressed in 1941, the *Dong-A Ilbo* alone was confiscated 489 times and its publication suspended on 63 occasions, in addition to the censorship in force.

The newspapers during those dark days thus struggled to keep alive the Korean sense of national and cultural identity. Forbidden to mention such topics as independence, or to criticize the Japanese in any way, they concentrated instead on stories intended to unify and encourage the Korean people.

After liberation from Japan, a free era of journalism came, though chaos began with the lifting of all restrictions on publication. Leftist papers burgeoned, as well as irresponsible journals and fly-by-night sheets. In 1964 the Korean newspapers offered to put teeth into a previously-organized Press Ethics Commission, and undertake self-policing activities. This system proved so successful that it was commended as an exemplary achievement at the London meeting of the International Press Institute in 1965.

Presently there are 32 daily newspapers in Korea, which include six vernacular national dailies—*Dong-A Ilbo, Chosun Ilbo, Kyunghyang Shinmoon, Hankook Ilbo, Joong-ang Ilbo,* and *Seoul Shinmun*—with a circulation of more than 600,000 copies each, two English dailies—*The Korea Herald* and *The Korea Times*— 10 regional papers, and 14 others.

Publication of other periodicals is also active. As of the end of May 1985, the country had 142 weeklies, among them the English-language weekly *Newsreview,* and the French-language weekly *Courrier de la Coree,* 989 monthlies, and 659 miscellaneous periodicals.

Radio and Television

The early stages of radio transmission in Korea were of course under the complete domination of the Japanese occupation authorities. Broadcasting began in Seoul in 1927, with a power output of just 1 kw, comprising news, weather, and market quotations in Japanese and Korean.

By 1933 there were both AM and short-wave facilities, with 10kw power. A separate Korean-language channel was granted, under strict supervision and subject to jamming. By the following year, Radio Seoul was beaming to Japan and Manchuria, and had its own studio orchestra, from which many notable local musicians emerged. The same year, Pusan was added to the national network; and by 1945 there were 17 outlets, with Seoul Central operating on 50kw.

With liberation, censorship and Japanese-oriented vocabulary vanished overnight. In 1952, the nation became a member of the International Telecommunications Union. The government-owned station, operating under the Office of Public Information (now the Ministry of Culture and Information), was called the

A television studio in Seoul.

Korea Broadcasting System (KBS). This became a publicly owned corporation in 1973.

After the inevitable disruptions and damages of the Korean War, KBS was expanded with the introduction of foreign language broadcasting and shortwave service. For overseas service Radio Korea presents 24 hours daily in Korean, English, Portuguese, French, German, Spanish, Chinese, Russian, Japanese, Italian, Indonesian, and Arabic through 20 different channels.

KBS Television began broadcasting on December 31, 1961. Unlike radio, costly television programs necessitate the charging of monthly service fees to owners of color TV sets. The total number of TV sets officially numbered 8,458,800 as of the end of April 1985, though the actual number is believed to be much greater. There are now two TV networks throughout the country, KBS and MBC.

Telephone and Telegram Service

In Korea, telephone service began in 1897 with a tieup between royal palaces in Seoul. Since then telephone service has expanded continually until in 1984 there were 5,594,973 telephone subscribers. The Ministry of Communications had opened international telephone service with 205 countries and areas as of 1984. With the operation of the fourth satellite telecommunication station in 1984, Korea is now linked directly with all parts of the world.

The number of foreign countries and areas having telex service with Korea increased to 260 at the end of 1984 and the number having telegraphic links reached 209.

Transportation

Parallel with Korea's economic development, its transportation industry has grown by leaps and bounds over the last decade and a half.

Even today, as in the early part of the past decade, new roads are constantly being built, new shipping routes explored, and new air corridors constantly sought and expanded—all to meet the demanding requirements of today and the challenges of tomorrow.

As of 1984, the combined length of the country's railroad network was 6,168 kilometers including 761.8 kilometers of double track railroads and 1,023 kilometers of electric railroads. Rolling stock included 459 diesel locomotives, 90 electric locomotives, 133 motor coaches and 370 electric motor cars. Suburban lines were electrified and connected to the Seoul subway system which went into operation in 1974.

The Seoul subway system carried 16.1 million passengers during its first year of operation, 34.3 million in 1975, 33.9 million in 1976, 66.5 million in 1979, and 212.6 million in 1984.

Some 8,310 buses transported 63.3 percent of Seoul's population in 1984, 34,434 taxis 15.5 percent and subways 10.3 percent. Efforts are continuously being made to reverse those figures and increase the percentage using subways. The subway system has been greatly expanded and now there are four lines, Nos. 1, 2, 3, and 4, in operation. A subway system has also been opened in Pusan, Korea's second largest city.

To cope with the ever increasing transportation needs of the nation's expanding industries, to expedite further industrial development and balanced regional growth and to bring every part of the country within a day's drive of each other, the construction of a network of expressways was initiated in 1968. As of 1984, seven expressways totalling 1,421km connected industrial complexes to urban centers, urban centers to tourist attractions, and the mountainous areas with the coasts. In 1984, 38.9 percent of the vehicles using the expressways were passenger cars, 14.3 percent were buses and 46.3 percent were trucks. The construction of an expressway to link Seoul with Taejŏn, a city in the central part of the country, was begun.

With the pressing demand for shorter travel time between inland points, new airports were built and in 1962 domestic air transportation entered an era that was to see its traffic register a 14-fold increase in 22 years. From 1970 to 1984 alone the total passengers carried jumped from 917,000 to 2,869,000 and cargo rose from 500 tons to 58,000 tons.

On the international scene, Korean Air (the nation's flag carrier) carried a total of 398,000 passengers and 25,700 tons of cargo on international flights during 1970, and 3,942,000 passengers and 302,000 tons of cargo during 1984. With the sole exception of 1974 Korean Air passenger transportation volume increased by an average of 25 percent a year.

Korean Air planes now fly to six different cities in Japan—Tokyo, Osaka, Kumamoto, Fukuoka, Nagoya and Niikata—and to Anchorage, Los Angeles, New York and Honolulu in the United States. On Southeast Asian routes, they make regular flights to Taipei, Hongkong, Singapore, Kuala Lumpur, Bangkok, Colombo and Manila, and on the Middle Eastern route to Jeddah and Dahran in Saudi Arabia and Bahrain, Kuwait,

Optical fibers are one of Korea's newest export items.

The port of Pusan, Korea's second largest city, has

Baghdad, Tripoli, and Abu Dhabi. Paris, Zurich, Amsterdam and Frankfurt are the European destinations of Korean Air. The government is improving airport facilities to accommodate the rapidly increasing international traffic. Cheju International Airport on Chejudo Island has already been expanded.

Kimpo International Airport, the main gateway to Korea, is undergoing a major expansion that will increase its annual passenger capacity from the present 4.8 million to 8.9 million in 1987, while its annual cargo capacity will rise from the present 320,000 met-

historically been the southern gateway to the nation.

ric tons to 540,000 tons. In addition, a new international airport will be opened in Ch'ŏngju in central Korea by 1992 after six years of construction.

The combined annual cargo handling capabilities at the nation's 21 trading ports is set to be increased from some 93 million tons in 1981 to 151 million tons by 1986 under vigorous port-expansion projects. The project for the largest port, Pusan, will double its annual cargo-handling capacity to 19 million tons and the maximum number of simultaneously docked ships to 78 from the present 35 by 1986.

Social Development
and Quality of Life

*Hospital ships call at remote islands regularly
for free medical service.*

Public Welfare

The living standards of the Korean people have substantially improved owing to the rapid economic growth since the early 1960s. Because of such growth, however, Korean society has had to undergo, in a short period, the kind of change that took place in developing countries of the West over several centuries. This has caused numerous socio-economic problems, including the disintegration of traditional values, a widespread sense of relative poverty and other difficulties accompanying industrialization, urbanization and the breakup of the extended family.

Keenly conscious of such conditions, the Korean Fifth Republic early adopted the building of a society capable of ensuring the well-being of all as a major national goal. The Constitution contains provisions to guarantee the welfare of all citizens and various laws have been enacted to promote the welfare of the handicapped and the aged and to establish a social welfare fund. Furthermore, the Fifth Five-Year Economic and Social Development Plan was designed to advance the goals of growth, stability, equity and harmony—all geared to promote the public welfare.

The scope of the medical insurance program, instituted only eight years ago, has been steadily expanded and now benefits 40 percent of the total population. At the same time, medical aid is being provided to eight percent of the population who are the most needy. The medical insurance system will be further expanded to benefit farmers, fishermen, small urban self-employed businessmen and others who are not currently covered. The goal is to have the entire population covered by medical insurance in the 1990s.

To provide inexpensive but good medical services to farming and fishing communities, public health centers and other public health facilities have been expanded, with a focus on primary health care. Medical facilities and personnel in rural areas will continue to be increased to meet rising demands for medical services due both to the implementation of medical insurance and improvements in the living standard. At the same time, public investments in special medical institutes, such as those treating adult diseases and mental illness, will be especially increased.

To help needy families stand on their own two feet rather than depend on public aid, a self-help program has been instituted to provide them with assistance in education and vocational training, and with small business loans, in addition to subsistence assistance. Institutes to accommodate those 65 or over, the handicapped, unfortunate youths, unmarried mothers and fatherless families are being expanded and social services for them are being reinforced and diversified.

An official committee has been set up to make preparations necessary to begin implementing a national pension fund during the latter half of the 1980s. The committee is to devise a national pension system suitable to the Korean situation that will coordinate and incorporate the current severance pay systems of business firms and the existing industrial accident insurance system.

One of the primary concerns of the government's public welfare policy is the alleviation of the chronic housing shortage. The population explosion, the heavy immigration to the cities and the increasing number of people living in nuclear families rather than in extended families has made the problem especially severe in the urban areas. The problem is exacerbated by the fact that housing costs have risen faster than incomes, making home ownership increasingly difficult for ordinary citizens.

In 1983, the nationwide housing shortage stood at 32.4 percent but in large urban areas it rose to 46.5 percent. To solve this housing problem, the Fifth Five-Year Economic and Social Development Plan called for 1,460,000 housing units to be built between 1982 and 1986. However in the first two years of the plan, actual construction fell short by 23,000 units, due to lot shortages in urban areas and a sharp increase in prices.

In an attempt to provide housing for non-owners, the government is encouraging private construction companies, the Korea Housing Corporation and local governments to build rental units as an alternative to the key-money units which require the downpayment of a large sum of money, the interest on which serves as rent. The advantage of the key-money system is that the occupant gets the principle back when he vacates the unit but the disadvantage is that key money is usually too large for low-income families to pay. The Korean Land Development Corporation will supply low-cost lots for the contruction of rental units and the National Housing Fund, established in 1981 to support the construction of public housing, will provide long-term low-interest loans.

Employment, Manpower Development and Income Distribution

Since the beginning of the 1980s, the growth of the economically active population has slowed down somewhat due to decreases in demand for farm labor because of mechanization, the increase in middle and high-school enrollment and the decreasing importance of labor-intensive light industries. In 1983, total employment was 14,515,000 while overall unemployment was 4.1 percent. The unemployment rate rose, however, to 4.4 percent in the non-farm sector.

Employment in the agriculture, forestry and fishery sector totaled 4,314,000 in 1983, a decrease of 309,000 from the previous year. In the mining and manufacturing sector it was 3,383,000, up 226,000, while in social overhead capital and other service sectors, it was 6,818,000, an increase of 174,000. There were rises in the number of professional, technological, managerial, administrative and clerical personnel during the year. The continuing flow of labor from primary to secondary and tertiary industries reflects the development of the nation's industrial structure.

The number of self-employed workers totaled 4,892,000 in 1983, a decrease of 27,000 from 1982 and the number of family members employed by self-employed workers dropped to 2,437,000, a fall of 200,000. On the other hand, the number of payroll employees rose to 7,184,000, up 318,000. The percent of payroll employees to total workers rose from 47.6 percent in 1982 to 49.5 percent in 1983, while the proportion of self-employed and family workers fell. These changes further reflect Korea's developing employment structure.

To meet the demands of the changing employment structure and prepare for an increasingly industrialized society, steps are being taken by both the government and private businesses to improve the quality of scientific and technical training to provide a sufficient number of highly trained workers. This has included steps to improve curricula and equipment at all levels from primary schools to universities, an increase in scholarship aid for graduate students, improvements in job placement services and salary levels, a substan-

Keenly conscious of the numerous socio-economic problems that have developed in parallel with the substantial improvements in living standards, the Fifth Republic early adopted the building of a society capable of ensuring the well-being of all as a major goal. In line with this policy, medical centers like the one seen here (above) and other facilities and services are being increased.

tial increase in vocational training facilities and compulsory training of 0.5 percent of all workers in private companies employing more than 300 persons.

Since the early 1950s, Korea has developed rapidly from an underdeveloped agricultural country into a newly industrializing nation. Of particular significance is the fact that during this process, Korea was largely able to avoid the usual trend of widening income disparities during the early stages of industrialization. Such disparities are usually caused by the rapid growth of the nonagricultural sector where income distribution is relatively more unequal than in the rural sector. Income distribution in Korea did deteriorate slightly during the period of rapid industrialization, especially from the mid-1970s, then the relative size of the farm population began to shrink quickly. But the degree of deteriorization has been much smaller than in most other countries in similar stages of industrialization.

This difference is attributed to various factors. First, rapid growth of education has enabled the rapid rise of the middle class. Second, the confrontation and competition with North Korea has stimulated concern about public welfare in the South, leading to vigorous policies of rural development, fairer taxation and greater social welfare for the poor.

The effective control of inflation since the beginning of the 1980s has stabilized income levels while stimulating high economic growth, thus laying the basis for increasingly more equitable distribution of income. Steps are also being taken to encourage faster upward readjustments of lower wages than of higher ones. This has resulted in the narrowing of wage gaps among different occupations and for workers with different levels of education.

The annual income of an average farm household is

roughly equivalent to that of an average urban wage earner and in several recent years has overtaken it. This is due largely to efforts to support agricultural prices at appropriate levels and to develop cash crops and off-farm income sources to boost earnings of the rural populace.

In sum, the pattern of income distribution in Korea has been improving since 1980 as a result of high growth combined with low inflation, decreasing wage differentials and a narrowing urban-rural income gap. An international comparison shows that income distribution in Korea is more equal than in all other developing countries, except Taiwan.

Equitable income distribution is essential to the social stability and economic vitality needed to achieve the country's development potential. Thus plans are being implemented to maintain an annual economic growth rate of 7-8 percent not only to provide jobs for 400,000-450,000 people who enter the labor market each year but also to reduce the 1985 unemployment rate of 4 percent. At the same time, middle school education is progressively being made free and compulsory. Programs to retrain workers in declining industries and vocational training of rural residents are being expanded. Employment agency services are also being enlarged and investment in employee welfare is being encouraged.

Assistance to the poor emphasizes vocational training and job placement services designed to enable them to find better-paying jobs. Steps are being taken to further reduce wage differentials, especially through hikes in the lowest wages. Moreover, assistance in housing, health and medical care and old-age security is being increased to aid lower-income people.

Measures are being taken to prevent excessive business concentration and foster the growth of small and medium industries which contribute significantly to employment. The tax system and banking services are being reformed to more effectively perform income redistributing functions. Steps are also being taken to minimize opportunities for windfall gains in order to promote a healthy work ethic.

Environmental Protection and Pollution Control

Deeply ingrained in Korean culture is a love of the land which Koreans often describe as a "land of rivers and mountains embroidered on silk." There are many clear rivers and lakes and steep wooded mountains bordering broad plains, all of which change with the four seasons. But the recent rapid economic growth with its concomitant industrialization and urbanization has had a detrimental effect on the environment. There has been marked contamination especially in the cities, rivers and coastal waters.

One of the four purposes of the Second Comprehensive National Physical Development Plan (1982-1991) is to protect the environment from pollution and conserve scenic areas, while at the same time promoting balanced economic development. Although the average level of air pollution in Seoul, Pusan and Ulsan has declined since 1981, the emission of pollutants in crowded areas of these cities still far exceeds permissible standards. Sulfur dioxide is the main air pollutant in Korea. In Seoul, the level of sulfur dioxide declined to 0.051 ppm in 1983 from 0.086 ppm in 1981. Taegu had 0.046 ppm of sulfur dioxide in 1983, up slightly from 0.039 ppm in 1982, and Ulsan, though a major industrial city, has kept its sulfur dioxide level at

0.33 ppm. However, these levels are relatively high compared with those of major cities in other countries.

Furthermore, the pollution of the nation's major rivers and of the sea water adjacent to industrial complexes on the east and south coasts has gradually increased. Industrial waste water, domestic sewage, night soil discharges and misuse of agrochemicals are the primary causes of this pollution. However, as the government's anti-pollution measures go into effect, the current level of biological oxygen demand (BOD) in the nation's major rivers will fall dramatically by 1986. For example, the Han-gang River at Noryangjin in Seoul had a BOD of 6.1 ppm in 1983, the worst pollution of any of the major rivers, but this is expected to drop to 3.0 ppm by 1986.

The Office of Environment is the central government agency for environmental protection. It is responsible for completing a long-term environmental protection plan by 1986 which will cover the Han-gang, Nakdonggang, Kŭmgang and Yŏngsan-gang rivers. This plan will set the goals for environmental protection until the year 2000, including the priority of anti-pollution projects. The agency will also implement a system to evaluate the environmental impact of major development projects which will require the development of new techniques for evaluating environmental impact, the expansion of environmental research and analysis programs, and increased research in environmental preservation technology. (See Forestry section of Economy chapter)

A new housing development reflects the city's

effort to keep up with its exploding population.

Women's Status

When the Yi Dynasty of the Chosŏn Kingdom was founded in 1392, bringing with it an adherence to strict Confucian mores, the role of Korean women was limited to the management of the large extended family and the producing of a male heir, and in all other things, she was expected to obey first her father and then her husband and sons. This concept has been so accepted in Korean culture that even today when family size has shrunk and women are well educated and have a great deal of free time, many still feel guilty about wanting to hold a job outside the home, and most who have successful careers admit that they would not have been able to do so without the support and understanding of their husbands.

There is evidence though that this was not always the case in Korea. Before 1392, women seemed to have had a great deal more freedom and in fact during the Shilla Kingdom (57 B.C.-A.D. 935), there were three reigning queens, one of which, Queen Sŏndŏk (r. 632-647), was credited with outstanding leadership and political ability.

Despite the limitation on women during the Yi Dynasty period which lasted until 1910, there were many women who distinguished themselves in literature, the arts, scholarship and household management. One of the most famous of these was the painter, calligrapher, poet, Shin Saimdang (1504-51). It is said that her paintings of plants, flowers and insects were so natural that the birds pecked at the insects. She was the mother of Yi I (Yulgok, 1536-84), one of the most renowned neo-Confucian scholars and a farsighted statesman. Such women provided positive examples that women could accomplish as much as men. They helped change the traditional idea that women were inferior to men and so laid the basis for the achievements of others.

Opportunities for women began to slowly open up at the end of the 19th century when Korea was finally opened to the outside world. The first girls school in Korea, Ewha Haktang, was opened in 1886 and from that small beginning, education for women has gradually increased until today Korean girls have equal educational opportunities with their brothers.

Women proved their courage and abilities during the struggle for national liberalization from the Japanese colonial rule (1910-45), even forming a Womens Righteous Army to fight the Japanese. However, it was only after the establishment of the Republic of Korea in 1948 that women won the clear constitutional right to equal education, to job opportunities and to participate in public life.

A series of economic development plans which began in the early 1960s and the Saemaŭl Undong (New Community Movement) which was started in the early 1970s to promote rural development have helped Korean society to grow rapidly. As a result, women have had increasingly greater opportunities to take part in economic activities and in 1983, there were 5.7 million working women. This figure amounted to 39.3 percent of the total work force. Despite this increase, the number of women holding policy-making positions in administration and management is still negligible.

Korean women today, however, are engaged in a wide variety of fields including manual work, education, medicine, science, engineering, scholarship, arts, literature, sports, and government. There are women company presidents, National Assembly members and cabinet ministers. This fact demonstrates that Korean women, given the opportunity, can develop their

potential and make significant contributions to public life. It cannot be denied, however, that it is nearly impossible for women to break into the male network of associations so vital to success in business or government.

Nevertheless, the increasing role of women and the changes in Korean society as a whole have brought the government to the realization that it must develop new policies for women. In 1983, the National Committee on Women's Policies was inaugurated by a presidential decree. Composed of representatives of various governmental ministries, the committee functions as a comprehensive deliberation body. The Korean Women's Development Institute was established by the National Assembly in April 1983 to make a comprehensive study of women's issues and to link its findings with government policies. The findings of its research program are made public and are used by the government as material for the formulation of new policies effecting women. At the request of the National Committee on Women's Policy, the Institute developed a Long-Range Plan for Women's Development and Guidelines for the Elimination of Discrimination Against Women, both of which have been adopted as official government policy.

Korean society has changed dramatically since the turn of the century and it can no longer afford not to utilize all its human resources. At the same time, Korean women have also changed and are increasingly ready and able to play a responsible role in all fields. As more and more women fight for the right to

Snow flurries lure a young couple to Tŏksugung Palace. Echoing the glory of Korea's past, the palace buildings nestle amid a landscape of modern buildings.

develop their skills to the fullest and make use of them and as society feels an increasing need for their talents, women will play an ever greater and more creative role in all parts of society.

Windsurfing on the Han-gang River in Seoul.

Leiŝure

Koreans play with the same energy and enthusiasm that, when applied to work, has given them the reputation of being the hardest working people in the world. It might also be said that they are the hardest playing people around. While economic growth and the rising standard of living has not resulted in as much leisure time as in many other countries, what time there is is used to the fullest, and the leisure industry is one of the fastest growing industries in the nation.

Besides the many museums, palaces, temples, royal tombs, parks and scenic and historic sites which have always been popular sites for family outings and picnics, Koreans today in increasing numbers are also spending much of their free time in some type of athletic pursuit. In the early hours of any weekday morning, men and women can be found crowding the tennis courts or jogging the streets, getting in a few hours of exercise before changing into business clothes and heading to the office. Such a love of sports was certainly behind the bid to host the 1988 Olympics and the resultant success in winning that right has added a measure of enthusiasm to all athletic endeavors. Besides tennis and running, Koreans by the hundreds and thousands take part in hiking, surf and fresh water fishing, swimming, golfing, skiing, water skiing, hunting, wind surfing, handball and various other individual or group sports, both organized and spontaneous. The spectator sports of soccer, baseball, basketball, volleyball, *ssirŭm* (Korean wrestling) and boxing all have an avid following.

At night Koreans have a wide variety of entertainment to choose from including traditional Korean and classical or modern Western performances at the Sejong Cultural Center, the National Theater and the National Classical Music Institute or dinner theaters, night clubs, discos, cabarets and beer halls featuring jazz, country, soul or rock 'n' roll. For movie goers, there are numerous theaters which show either domestic or European and American films. There are also many small theater groups which stage plays by Korean playwrights and translations of well-known foreign works.

The sound of a kŏmun-go, a six-string Korean zither, echoes through a traditional Korean garden.

Customs
and
Traditions

Korea is a country blending change and tradition. In both the city and the countryside the appearance of Korea is changing with great speed but beneath this transformation of society is a stability born of centuries-old traditions and customs which while modified to fit a new society still have great meaning and a powerful influence.

Confucianism is mixed with the shamanism and animism that came before and Western philosophical concepts that came after, and is now so ingrained into the Korean psyche that it is difficult to tell what in Korean life is truly Confucian and what is not. People do not usually think of themselves as Confucian, though the natural Korean way to do things is largely the Confucian way. This is reflected in social life, in the relations of family members, between "seniors" and "juniors," between men and women, and between friends. It is reflected in the hierarchy of social relations, in the respect felt toward the elderly, in the desire for education, in ceremonies to commemorate the deceased, and in the continuing influence of the extended family, even though increasingly—at least in the city—the living unit is a nuclear family. Filial piety and patriotism are cardinal virtues taught all children.

Group ties are very strong in Korea, and it is expected that the individual will work hard to contribute to the group, even, if necessary, at the expense of his personal desires.

Names

Koreans almost universally have three names: the family name or surname placed first, and a name identifying the generation, ordinarily the same for all male members of a clan, alternating in each generation to second or third place with the given or personal name.

Sometimes Koreans when writing their names in the Western or Roman alphabet will invert the word order and place the family name last, as Westerners do. This can lead to confusion, however, since many Occidentals know about the traditional word order of Oriental names, and will thus still misidentify the family name by reinverting the inverted order.

A good rule of thumb to bear in mind is that only a few family names cover the vast majority of all Koreans. If you see the names Kim, Lee, Pak, Ahn, Chang, Cho, Choe, Chung, Han, Kang, Ku, Ko, Im, Oh, Noh, Shin, Yu or Yun, you can be fairly sure that it is the family name, whether it appears as the first or third word in the sequence. There are, however, about 300 family names in Korea. A woman does not change her name when she marries.

Clothing

Nowadays in the streets of Korean cities one sees most of the people wearing Western clothing. But, some people—especially women—wear both Korean and Western clothing depending on convenience and the occasion.

The traditional male costume consists of a short, loose shirt-jacket with long, full sleeves and wide, baggy trousers which are tied at the ankle. The jacket is crossed over in the front and tied with a half bow. A vest may also be worn. In place of the vest, well-to-do men would often wear a jacket, slightly longer than the

The graceful wing-tipped tiled roofs of the traditional L-shaped

houses are a vestige of a quickly passing way of life.

shirt and also tied in the front with a half bow. In cool weather a long coat of the same basic design is also worn. The female costume consists of a very short, flared blouse crossed in the front and tied with long ribbons, and a long, high-waisted skirt. Women also use long coats on cold days.

Housing

Lately, many Koreans in big cities have taken to living in Western-style houses or apartments. But still many urban houses and almost all of those in the countryside embody the traditional style. The building is often one-story, with walls of brick, or cement building blocks. The roof is made of tiles or corrugated zinc or slate.

The most distinctive aspect of a Korean house is its age-old "radiant heating" system, called *ondol*. Under the floor of the room run stone flues that carry heat from the kitchen fire or external ground-level grates and heat the floors most efficiently.

Food

Rice, either plain or cooked with other grains, is the main dish at all Korean meals. Rice is accompanied by a variety of side-dishes. Favorite side-dishes include bean-paste soup, pickled cabbage called *kimchi*, roasted beef and fish, and steamed and seasoned vegetables. Soy sauce, soybean paste, red pepper paste, ginger root, sesame oil and sesame seeds are other seasonings which are essential to Korean food.

Food is not eaten in courses but served all at once and eaten together. Among favorite dishes are *pulgogi*, strips of beef roasted over a brazier at the table after being marinated in a mixture of soy sauce, sesame oil, sesame seeds, garlic, green onions and other seasonings; and *shinsŏllo*, a court dish combining meat, eggs, nuts and vegetables artistically arranged in a special chafing dish used just for this purpose.

Family Occasions

The two most important birthdays in the life of a Korean are the first and 60th. At the first birthday party (*tol*), the child is dressed in a colorful traditional costume and sits amidst piles of rice cakes, cookies and fruits.

At 60, a man was considered to have completed the cycle of active life. This is not the case now but the 60th birthday, or *hwankap*, is still a landmark in life that is an occasion of family festivity. On this day, one is offered rich food and drinks, and receives best wishes for longevity and felicity from one's children and grandchildren. Relatives and acquaintances are invited to a grand banquet.

Old-style Confucian funerals were elaborate rituals involving solemn processions. When the coffin is placed in the grave, a mound about one meter high is made over it. The mound is sodded later to keep it from eroding. It is usual to mark the grave with a tombstone and sometimes with a stone tablet and tomb pillars. These customs have gradually become simplified, as in

A traditional Korean wedding.

the case of weddings and *hwankap* parties, as a result of a social campaign, for such ceremonies were often expensive.

Old-fashioned wedding ceremonies, with the elaborately-costumed groom riding a pony to the house of the bride to share with her ceremonial sips of wine at their first meeting, are rarely encountered now. Instead, an institution has grown up in cities and towns

214

called the wedding hall, where an auditorium—complete with music and flowers, and with bridal gowns and dress suits for hire—is available.

Traditional Games

Yut: This old-style New Year's game employs a playing board on which is drawn a diagram with "Start" and "Home," as in many modern Western games. Four sticks, with one side rounded and one side flat, function somewhat like dice: they are thrown into the air and tallied according to which side falls uppermost. Players or teams take turns and move their counters according to the fall of the sticks. The game, simple in essence, evokes a great deal of boisterous enthusiasm among holiday players.

Paduk: This Korean game is called *"go"* in Japan. Historic records show that it was known in Korea nearly 2,000 years ago. Two players face each other over a board drawn in squares; one player has white counters and the other black. The object is to "surround" the enemy pieces and render them helpless. Rules are simple but strategies complex. It is notable that the action takes place on the intersection of lines, not in the squares, as in Western board games. *Paduk* is a "lifetime preoccupation" for many, like chess; there are championships, televised tournaments, and publications endlessly analyzing master moves and hypothetical games.

Changgi: Changgi is yet one more variation on the immemorially ancient prototype of chess said to have been devised in Mesopotamia as much as 4,500 years

ago. Koreans play a version close to the Chinese, and somewhat different from the Japanese. The board is divided by 10 horizontal and nine vertical lines, and the object of the king and other battle pieces is to keep the queen immobilized and protected. Each player has 16 pieces of seven different types and the game usually ends in checkmate, like European chess.

Seesaw: The seesaw is a girls' game played on lunar New Year's Day, very early in spring. The board is set on a low stone or bag filled with rice straw; the players stand upright, jump in the air, and come down hard. It may have begun in order to give girls a fleeting glimpse of the world outside their walled yard, back in the days when ladies were never permitted to leave home.

Kite Flying: Kites in Korea were flown early in spring, during the First Month of the lunar calendar. Kite flying was often competitive, each youthful player trying to cut the string of an opponent by crossing the strings in mid-air. Sometimes powdered glass was glued to the string to make it more formidable. At the end of the kite-flying month, boys used to write "Away Evil, Come Blessings," and release their kites to bear away the family's bad luck.

Swinging: Like the seesaw, a swing in Korea was for girls originally, and swinging took place standing up. The pastime was associated with New Year's Day, *Tano,* and *Chusŏk* (See the section on holidays).

When snow blankets the low hills of Korea, little boys in traditional Korean attire get ready to go kite flying during the Lunar New Year's holidays.

217

Arts

*Wearing the brilliant court musicians'
dress, the National Classical Music
Institute's musicians preserve and
perform the old court music.*

Some commentators have attempted to compare or contrast the arts of the three principal North Asian nations with the generalization that Chinese art appears massive and ornate, that of the Japanese seems dainty and refined, while the arts of Korea give an impression of unpolished simplicity and rude strength. Such formulas may be useful if it is carefully borne in mind that the generalization will not necessarily fit for all the arts or all the periods in the histories of any of the three countries.

With the establishment of the Republic of Korea, the compiling of a list of National Treasures was begun. These might be art objects, antique handicraft items, buildings, or such intangible treasures as dances, folk dramas, music, and individual performers or craftsmen connected with these.

The National Treasures, now numbering 230, are guaranteed government preservation and fostering. In recent years, activities directed toward restoration and protection of the National Treasures have been stepped up under the aegis of the Ministry of Culture and Information.

Painting and Calligraphy

Tomb murals from the Koguryŏ Kingdom (37 B.C.-A.D. 668) are the earliest surviving examples of Korean painting. The mythological beasts depicted in some of these show a fantastic imagination and wild abandon

Cats and Sparrows, *by Pyŏn Sang-byŏk (early 18th century), a professional painter who served the royal court and mainly painted portraits of kings and great Confucian statesmen.*

that seems already somehow quintessentially Korean.

Then comes a long gap caused by the fragility of early paintings done on cloth, wood, or mud-plaster walls. Not until the Chosŏn Kingdom are there enough extant paintings to generalize about.

In Chosŏn Kingdom days there were two classes of artists. The first included professionals employed by the court for portraits, decorative landscape and genre paintings, and amateurs, actually highly cultivated scholar-poets who also painted and practiced calligraphy. The latter are at least as esteemed by modern experts as the former, though no scholar-artist of the old days would have demeaned himself to the level of a mere artisan by exhibiting his work publicly. The style of painting of this group was somewhat influenced by the Chinese, but there is a recognizable Korean flavor to the humorous animal pictures, the scroll paintings of dreamlike, mist-clad mountains, and the sharply-observed sketches of modern life dashed off with deceptive ease in brush and ink. The second group included numerous unnamed folk artists who created a unique Korean art reflecting the life and vitality of the common people, and employing an elaborate symbolism based on Chinese traditions. Korean folk art is just beginning to be appreciated for its rich contribution to the arts of Korea.

Calligraphy, or brush writing, is a definite art form in Korea, as it is in China and Japan. Calligraphy in Korea has exerted a strong influence on social and cultural life, and even today it is respected as an art.

With the 20th century, Western art trends came to Korea—influencing, but not submerging, the still-active tradition of Oriental-style painting. Many Korean artists, using Occidental techniques, have begun to look back into Korean mythology and history for subjects and inspiration.

A hanging scroll by calligrapher, Kim Chong-hui (1786-1857).

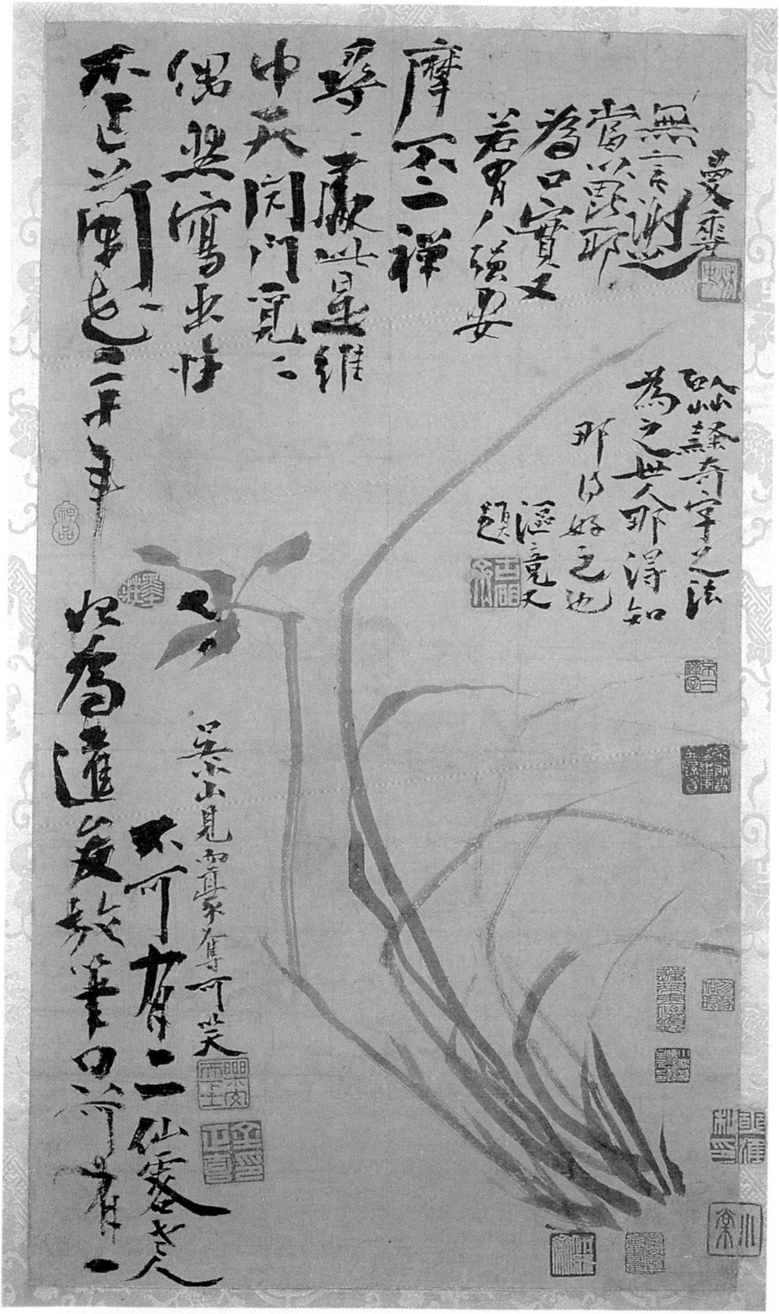

Small holes show that this 12th-century Koryŏ monkey and baby was used as a water dropper.

Sculpture, Architecture and Ceramics

Early sculpture in Korea is identified with the inflow of Buddhism. Images of Buddha in his various incarnations, and the Buddhist saints and minor deities are the main subjects, reaching breathtaking heights of artistry during the Unified Shilla period, exemplified by the granite figures of the Sŏkkuram Grotto shrine, erected in 752 near Kyŏngju. Other materials used for large images include iron, bronze, and gilded wood. Smaller figures might be of gilt bronze, soapstone, gold or glazed clay.

Here it may be proper to mention the striking beauty of certain carved jade ornaments; the grandiose originality of the openwork Shilla gold crowns; and the ethereal grace of pictorial patterns chased in relief on the surface of certain huge cast bronze bells. When Buddhism lost its political sway in the Chosŏn Kingdom, sculpture as an art practically disappeared, except local and imitative items for temple use.

Temples and official buildings such as palaces follow the basic Chinese design in lintel style: horizontal wooden beams supported on wooden posts. Walls might be of wood or clay and lime wattle. Some castles, tombs and pagodas were made of granite. Unlike Chinese or Japanese architecture, the Korean roof curves up at both corners, and both ends of the roof ridge curve up also. Again, Buddhist influence by way of China is predominant up to the time of the Chosŏn Kingdom, when over-elaborate decoration bespoke the decadence of the era.

Naturally, not many original wooden structures remain from early times. Warfare and accidental fires have decimated the larger portion of such buildings and gates, especially those over 500 years old. There are, however, careful reconstructions of the originals.

Korean ceramics, especially the glazed celadon utensils of the Koryŏ Kingdom (935-1392), are by far the most famous single class of art objects the nation has produced. Long valued and sought after in the West not only for their artistic beauty but for their high craftsmanship, Koryŏ celadon can be imitated but not duplicated today. The composition of the glaze and the firing techniques of the Koryŏ potters were forgotten even by the Chosŏn Kingdom, though Chosŏn white porcelains with underglaze designs were worthy successors. Invading Japanese troops in 1592 kidnapped Korean potters to begin the Japanese fine ceramics industry, testimony to the preeminence assigned to Korea's ceramic arts.

The earlier earthenware pots of Shilla and the Three Kingdoms have their admirers, too, who favor their simplicity and unrefined grace above more sophisticated products.

Prose and Poetry

Early Korean literature was influenced by China in terms of theme and style. However, certain Korean strains can be observed throughout the nation's literary history: a spirit of flexible resilience and humorous bravado in the face of adversity balanced by nostalgia and love of nature and allied with an uneasy sense of the transitory and fragile quality of life.

The most popular form of all, the brief lyric verses known as *shijo*, appeared only in late Koryŏ times. These highly formal poems were often improvised for special occasions, and the older examples at least were intended to be chanted or sung, belonging as much to music as to literature. *Shijo* captured the Korean imagination, and are written to the present day, now usually as straight literary pieces. During the Chosŏn Kingdom, long narrative poems which had also dominated in Koryŏ remained popular. All these were diversions of the scholars and nobility, and were usually written in Chinese characters.

Among the common people, a traveling minstrel often chanted old stories by rote to drum accompaniment. These lengthy quasi-operatic epics were called *p'ansori* and in recent years have been adapted as multicharacter stage pieces.

Historical compilations like the *Samguksagi* and *Samgukyusa* were filled with old tales and legends. In mid-Koryŏ times, collections of such narratives, anecdotes, and piquant episodes presaged the development of the classic novels of the Chosŏn period. Korea's most durable love story, *Chunhyangjŏn,* often filmed and dramatized, appeared in the late 18th century, and contains elements of social protest. Many of the classic novels are anonymous, since fiction, unlike poetry, was considered a frivolous pastime for an educated man.

It remains to mention that pure scholars and philosophically inclined monks enriched Korean literature through the ages with essays and extended prose works on elevated subjects, many of which are still read and admired.

As in the case of the other arts, Western influences began to infiltrate around the turn of the century. Original modern novels, essays, and verse now crowd the literary marketplace, along with translations of popular and classic Occidental books.

A fair amount of Korean literature has recently been translated into Western languages, mostly English. In addition, a surprising number of Korean authors,

Many ancient court dances have been rearranged to blend a modern mood

including a number of expatriates, have begun to write original works in English and other European languages.

Music and Dance

If Koreans are known by one trait among foreigners, it is for their love of, and proficiency in the arts of music and dance. Native Korean music comprises *aak* (Confucian ritual music), *tangak* and *hyangak* (court ceremonial music of Chinese and local origin respectively), and vocal music. To these must be added Buddhist chants and the folk music and farmers bands of the common people.

Court music is slow, solemn, and complex in its

*and temperament with traditional
dance elements.*

intertwining of long, elaborately decorated melodic lines. Ancient instruments, many adapted from Chinese prototypes, include plucked-string zithers, flutes and double reeds, and a variety of percussion. The human voice is traditionally accompanied by drum only, to mark the beat. The dances that go with some of the court music are likewise stately and highly stylized. Folk music, in contrast, is usually fast and lively, with vigorous, athletic dancing. Irregular rhythms in compound triple time predominate. Some of the same instruments are used, but folk music relies largely on metal gongs, the hourglass-shaped drum called the *changgo*, and a loud, trumpet-like oboe. Modern composers, including some foreign experts, have notated, adapted, and paraphrased portions of the old music.

Western music caught on rapidly after the introduction of Western culture in the late 19th century. Today there are several symphony orchestras, opera compan-

The Korea Philharmonic Orchestra performs regularly

and has won great popularity among music lovers.

ies, and music colleges in Korea. Recitals by foreign and local artists are frequent and well attended. Popular music with a Korean flavor is heard everywhere, and at parties or picnics the main entertainment is impromptu solo singing or dancing by all the participants in turn.

With so much musical interest and activity, it is not surprising that a dozen or more younger Korean musicians have already gained high reputation abroad as top performers in both the concert and entertainment fields. Serious Korean composers have turned out many ambitious works heard locally, some based on traditional elements, some following international or avant-garde models.

Drama and Cinema

The common people in Korea have always enjoyed a thriving tradition of mask plays: half-pantomime, half-ballet featuring earthy satire and horseplay. Aside from these and the minstrel-like *p'ansori* performers (See Literature), there has not been a strong theatrical tradition in Korea. After liberation in 1945, modern drama was briefly popular, but soon dwindled in the face of competition from radio, films, and finally television. In recent years there have been frequent short runs in Seoul and other major cities of plays ranging from local efforts to Western classics, musicals, and operas. An annual drama festival is sponsored by the Korean Culture and Arts Foundation to encourage new talent among playwrights, directors and actors.

Korea's first film was made in 1919. Cinema flourished until 1938, when political conditions caused its demise. It was not until 1955, with government assistance and newly-imported modern equipment, that Korean films began to come of age.

The National Museum

The National Museum of Korea grew out of the Yi Royal Household Museum, organized in 1908, and an archaeological collection established in 1915, during Japanese rule. With liberation from Japan in 1945, these exhibits were amalgamated as the National Museum of Korea, the headquarters of which is in Seoul.

Over the years, a number of branch museums have been set up in provincial centers where regional finds and special collections centering on one historic period or cultural epoch are displayed. The oldest branch is in Kyŏngju, ancient capital of the Shilla Kingdom, and there are others in Puyŏ and Kongju, both former capitals of the Paekche Kingdom, Chinju and Kwangju. But naturally the central museum in Seoul has had first choice of the nation's important artifacts, and the longest period of activity in which to enlarge its collections.

A total of 107,288 objects (as of April 1985) are in all the national museums, comprising all fields, from prehistoric archaeological relics to paintings and pottery of the last century. The collections are attractively arranged and displayed, with placards in English, in spacious well-lit buildings. The National Museum has been responsible for arranging several important international travelling exhibits.

Religions

An outdoor candlelight service at Myŏngdong Cathedral in Seoul.

Today's Korea is a melting pot of world religons, Oriental and Occidental, where the integrity of each individual's freedom to believe, or not to believe, what he pleases is assured by constitutional guarantees. Of course, the advent of ancient Asian religions in Korea preceded the proselytizing of faiths from distant regions and disparate cultures. And Korea, in fact, had its own unique religion from prehistoric times, a form of animism or nature worship involving a national foundation myth that told of a son of the supreme deity who descended to earth, married a bear-totem woman and founded the first Korean state.

Animism persisted in coloring the Korean versions of other world religions as they reached the peninsula, and survives today in the continuing reliance by simple rural people on the ceremonies conducted by shamans, or *mudang*, to ward off bad luck, insure success, and cure illnesses by invoking the power of nature spirits, or placating the vengeful wrath of ancestral spirits with some grievance against their descendants.

Buddhism

The earliest foreign religion to attain wide acceptance in Korea was Buddhism, which entered the country via Chinese and Indian missionaries around 372. After a period of rejection by the Shilla government, the new faith was accepted due to alleged miracles performed by saintly monks. When the royal fam-

A monk offers a silent prayer before the great Buddha at Pulguksa Temple in Kyŏngju. The Tabot'ap pagoda in the terraced courtyard is of unsurpassed beauty.

ily adopted Buddhism, the rest of the country rapidly followed suit. Soon the hillsides of Korea erupted in temples, shrines, hermitages, pagodas and stone *miruk* images. Buddhist architecture, sculpture, painting and theological scholarship flourished.

The fingerprint of a persisting animism within the Buddhist system is still found at nearly all Buddhist temples, where a small shrine is devoted to the Mountain Spirit and his attendant tiger, the old national totem animal. This subsidiary shrine is often the object of more fervent devotion than the main Buddhist sanctuary with its stately gilt images.

Buddhism was blamed, rightly or wrongly, for political reverses suffered by Korea during the Koryŏ Kingdom, and when the Yi family took power in 1392, the Buddhist clergy were banished from the capital and the religion disestablished.

In recent years Buddhism has experienced a revival in Korea, modernizing its outlook, seeking ties with sister movements in other countries, and espousing ideals of social service and ecumenical cooperation like other world religions.

Avowed Buddhist believers among Koreans number some 7,507,059. There are 7,244 accredited temples with 22,260 clergy, male and female.

Buddha's Birthday, the eighth day of the Fourth Month by the lunar calendar is a national holiday, and there are Buddhist chaplains serving with the armed forces.

Confucianism

There is endless argument over whether the tenets

238

of the Chinese sage Confucius and the social institutions based on them constitute a religion or not. It is true that there is no deity in the Confucian system (Heaven when referred to represents Fate or Things As They Are or the Moral Imperative of Kant, not a personified god), and no cosmogony.

On the other hand, Confucianism does embrace a moral and ethical system, a philosophy of life and interpersonal relations, a code of conduct, and a method of government, all viable enough to have taken the place of more orthodox religious beliefs in China for thousands of years, and the same held true in Korea.

The philosophy of Confucius entered Korea at nearly the same time as the religion of Buddha, and had a strong influence on social and governmental institutions. But it was not until the establishment of the Chosŏn Kingdom and its ousting of Buddhism from political influence in the late 14th century that Confucianism was elevated to the status of state cult, a position left vacant by the disestablishment of Buddhism.

Education in the Chinese classics, and particularly the ethical and philosophical books of Confucius, became the sole basis of education; and erudition represented the only path to social and political success. State examinations, which many failed and took over and over again for years while dependent on their families for support as students, determined the criteria for advancement of the scholar-administrator, the only career which a man of talent and breeding could honorably pursue.

Confucianism at best did insure stability and security within the system, but was woefully inadequate to meet challenges from outside, whether military, political or social. Korea thus became the "Hermit Kingdom" until the painful period late in the 19th century when the old system went into protracted death agonies due to overwhelming incursions from Japan and the Western powers.

To this day, many aspects of Confucianism remain central to the Korean character. As of 1983, Confucianism had 232 meeting places; 11,828 moral teachers and 786,955 adherents. A memorial ceremony in honor of Confucius and his principal disciples is held twice a year, in spring and fall, at Seoul's Sŏnggyungwan Shrine.

Christianity

Christianity began in Korea with the indirect influence of Western ideas brought back from China by Korean tributary emissaires, who met Catholic missionaries in Peking. The earliest such recorded contact occurred in 1783.

For some years there was no priest to serve the Korean converts-by-hearsay; when foreign missionaries entered the country by stealth and ordained Korean clergy, so that the religion began to grow in influence, it suffered severe persecution from a dogmatically Confucian government, which regarded the foreign creed as little better than devil worship. Nevertheless, by 1865 there were an estimated 20,000 Catholic converts in Korea. At this point the most severe persecutions began, not coincidentally at a time when the government was locked in a last-ditch struggle to drive off all foreign influence. Thousands of converts died, 93 of whom were canonized by Pope John Paul II when he visited Korea from May 3-7, 1984. (Ten

Status of Religions

(As of 1983)

Religion	Churches	Clergymen	Followers
Buddhism	7,244	22,260	7,507,059
Confucianism	232	11,828	786,955
Catholicism	2,342	4,529	1,590,625
Protestantism	21,243	31,740	5,337,308
Chŏndogyo	249	3,264	52,530
Wŏnbulgyo	344	3,921	96,333
Others	791	5,893	216,809
Total	32,445	83,435	15,587,619

French missionaries were also canonized at the same time.)

Then came the treaties with Western governments signed under pressure in 1882, and suddenly Korea was wide open as a mission territory, with the lives and rights of missionaries and converts guaranteed by the government, however unwillingly. Following the arrival of the first Protestant missionaries in 1885, the nation rapidly became one of the most active Christian mission fields worldwide. The reasons were not entirely involved with theology, although it is certainly true that the discrediting and demise of Confucianism as a formal philosophic system left a vacuum in Korean moral

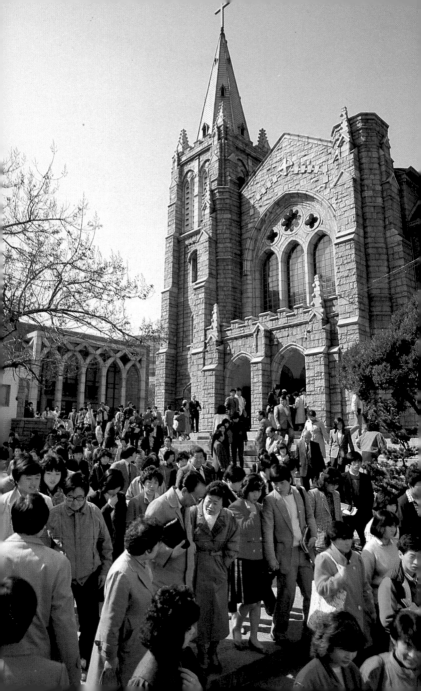

A church, a mosque and a pagoda symbolize the variety of religious experiences available to Koreans. There are more than 250 religious sects, some with as few as 10 members and others with as many as a million.

values that cried out to be filled. Perhaps more important was the fact that the missionaries championed
modern education, the Western work ethic, social
mobility, the comforts of affluent Western society, and
the humanistic and democratic ideals of the liberal par-
liamentarian nations, and thus became a rallying point
for resistance to Japanese encroachment, both before
and after Korea's annexation by Japan.

Christianity thus recruited to its ranks many of the
brightest and most progressive youths in Korean society, with the result that a disproportionate number of
the nation's leaders and shapers have been Christians
since the early years of the century. Today there are
1,590,625 Catholic believers, 2,342 Catholic churches, and 4,529 priests in Korea and 5,337,308 Protestant believers, 21,243 churches, and 31,740
ministers.

Islam

The Muslim religion was introduced into Korea during the Korean War by chaplains of the Turkish military
forces that fought under the United Nations banner in
1950-1953. Islam is thus the most recent of the world
religions to reach Korea's shore.

The Korean Muslim Federation was inaugurated as
recently as 1960, and conversion was speeded up by
the comparatively large numbers of Korean engineers
and laborers who since the early 1970s have been
serving in Middle Eastern countries on construction
projects undertaken by Korean firms.

A mosque in traditional architectural design was
dedicated in Seoul in May 1976 at a service attended

by more than 40 prominent leaders from the Islamic world who had assisted the project and taken a keen interest in the Muslim movement in Korea. A second and third mosque have been dedicated in Pusan and Kwangju (Kyŏnggi-do Province).

Indigenous Religions

During the chaotic last years of the 19th century, many native religious movements emerged, calling for social reform, whether through progressive or reactionary policies, but always via divine intervention of a charismatic leader or savior. Most of these movements were shortlived, but a few had significant historic roles to play, and some survive with significant membership today.

Chŏndogyo (Tonghak)
Korea underwent two great social upheavals in the 1860s: popular unrest caused by an oppressive ruling class and the introduction of Catholicism, followed by the expansion of Western influence. Around this time a native religion called *Tonghak* was founded by Ch'oe Che-u, a country scholar and minor aristocrat.

Tonghak held that heaven and man were indivisible and that all men were equal. Calling itself "Eastern learning," *Tonghak* rejected Catholicism as "Western learning," and dismissed the ancient cults, along with Confucianism, Buddhism and Taoism as having lost their essence. It maintained paradise belonged here and now—a terrestrial rather than celestial "Kingdom of Heaven."

Ch'oe Che-u's ideas influenced the people, and despite his martyrdom in 1864, *Tonghak* spread, mostly through the southern provinces. The result was a rural uprising that shook the weak central government. For a while in 1894, *Tonghak* armies controlled large parts

Young students perform an ancient dance as part of Sŏkchŏnje, *a ceremony commemorating Confucius' birthday.*

of southern Korea before they were crushed by government and Japanese troops.

After its founder was executed for heresy, *Tonghak* influence waned, although it survived under the new name of *Chŏndogyo*, and with a purely religious-nationalist approach survives to this day. At the time of the Samil Independent Movement in 1919, *Chŏndogyo* and Protestant Christians were particularly active.

Wonbulgyo

Wonbulgyo was founded in Yŏnggwang, Chŏllanam-do by So Tae-san (Park Chung-bin) in March 1916. The *Wonbulgyo* creed is based on the harmony of Buddhist teachings and the individual's beliefs.

Taejonggyo

Taejonggyo, Korea's oldest religion, is about 4,000 years old and embodies a national myth. The central concept is that of a triune god: creator, teacher and temporal king, whose name is Hanŭl. This god took human form in the person of Tan-gun, the father, teacher and king of the Korean people, who descended from heaven. This event is supposed to have happened in 2333 B.C., and until recent times Korean calendars were reckoned from this year.

Tan-gun established rituals for offering prayers of praise and propitiation to heaven. These rituals became strongly established among nobles and commoners alike by the end of the Three Kingdoms period, but with the introduction of foreign religions, purity in the practice of *Taejonggyo* gradually declined. By the 15th century, this cult had practically disappeared, but the resurgence of Korean nationalism in the late 19th and 20th centuries led to the appearance of several sects claiming to represent a revival of this ancient religion.

Sports

The main stadium of the Seoul Sports Complex where many of the events of the '88 Olympics will be held.

Koreans are by nature an extroverted, active, fun-loving people who pursue sports with the same vigor and singleminded determination that they devote to work. Children are encouraged from an early age to undertake physical development and to seek excellence in competitive athletic events, whether individually or as team members.

Spectator sports are increasingly popular, but non-competitive activities like hiking, mountain climbing, fishing, hunting and water sports are also pursued with the dedication of the serious hobbyist. There has also been a recent revival of traditional sports and games.

Although a Korean marathon runner Son Ki-chŏng won a medal in the 1936 Berlin Olympics, competing out of necessity under the Japanese flag, Korea participated in the international games under its own flag for the first time in London in 1948. Since then the nation's athletes have been consistently bettering their Olympic records, so that in the 1984 Los Angeles games they won six gold medals, six silver, and seven bronze, ranking 10th out of a field of 140.

Korean athletes shone in the 9th Asian Games in New Delhi by capturing 28 gold, 28 silver and 37 bronze medals to rank third after China and Japan, participating in 20 of the 21 events.

In 1977, an 18-member Korean Alpine team scaled Mt. Everest, and set a record as the first group to do so so early in the climbing season.

The government has taken a strong interest in fostering sports, both to promote physical fitness and to enhance national prestige by improved performance at international events. An 18-acre training site with the latest equipment and facilities for various athletic games has been set up in the outskirts of Seoul. In 1972 the National Sports Promotion Foundation was set up, charged with the responsibility for raising and administering funds for athletic activities. Furthermore, the government inaugurated the Ministry of Sports on March 20, 1982 in an effort to better coordinate government support for various sports programs.

Asian and Olympic Games in Seoul

1981 was a memorable year in the history of Korea's sports. The country was selected to host the 24th Summer Olympiad in 1988 and also the Asian Games in 1986. At its 84th general assembly held in Baden-Baden, West Germany in September 1981, the International Olympic Committee chose Seoul as the venue for the 1988 Summer Olympics. Following that decision, the Seoul Olympic Organizing Committee (SLOOC) was organized and, in cooperation with the government and the public, it began to build and renovate the necessary facilities for the two events. In addition to the Seoul Olympic Stadium seating 100,000, which was dedicated in September 1984, there will be 30 other sites, many of which are municipal or university facilities that are being brought up to Olympic standards.

A seven-story press center will be in operation for the 9,000 journalists, broadcasters, cameramen and communication technicians who are expected to cover the Seoul Olympics. It will offer large working areas, comprehensive telecommunication facilities, interview rooms with 700 seats, photo labs, conference rooms, restaurants and snack bars and other facilities.

During the Olympics, the Seoul Olympic Organizing Committee will also be sponsoring a series of cultural events. The whole gamut of Korean art forms, both

traditional and modern, will be demonstrated in these events, including music, dance, dramas, folk arts and fine arts; and many national treasures will be on display. Artists and performers from other Olympic nations will also be invited to participate, making it a truly international festival. Some of the planned events include an Olympic eve grand concert, an exhibit of Korea's national treasures, an exhibit of folk art, a festival of performing arts, the International Folklore Festival, the Seoul International Song Festival and an international film festival. These events will be held in Seoul and provincial cities. The Seoul Olympic Organizing Committee has commissioned representative Korean artists and architects to create monuments and sculptures and other artistic works to enhance the city for the Olympics.

Korea is the second nation in Asia and the first developing country to host the Olympics. It is thus important not only for Koreans but for the people of all developing countries. While providing every necessity and comfort for the athletes and while making the Olympics a successful athletic event and a great cultural experience, Korea intends to make this the most efficient and economically sound Olympics in history: thereby providing an example which other developing countries could follow in future years. By so doing, the Olympics will truly become a world event and not simply the exclusive preserve of the advanced countries.

The Asian Games Federation also selected Seoul as the site of the 1986 Asian Games. The selection came

Ha Hyung-ju, a 1984 Los Angeles Olympic gold medalist, defeated his Brazilian opponent to win the gold in the half-heavy (95kg) judo division at the 1985 Universiade in Kobe, Japan.

at the general assembly of the Federation held in New Delhi on November 26, 1981.

The government of the Republic of Korea has pledged to extend all available support to Seoul's hosting of the games and to welcome participants from all countries around the world regardless of any difference in ideologies, race and religions.

Popular Sports

Soccer: The most popular sport in Korea today is undoubtedly soccer, which was introduced in 1882 by the crew of a visiting British warship. Today, Korea has one of the best teams in Asia. The President's Cup Football Tournament was begun in 1971 and has since attracted numerous teams to Korea. In 1985, for example, it drew teams from Bahrain, Iraq, Thailand, Malaysia, Belgium, Brazil, Argentina and Uruguay. The first professional team was formed in 1980 and by 1984 there were six professional teams which compete in a pennant race each year.

Baseball: This popular American game was introduced to Korea, strangely enough, by YMCA staff and students at the German Language Institute in Seoul in 1906. At present, high school leagues are extremely active, and college leagues are increasingly popular. In 1982, the Korean team was the champion in the 27th World Baseball Championship in Seoul. With the formation in March 1982 of a professional baseball league with six teams, baseball fever has swept the country, especially among young fans who can be seen in their baseball uniforms pitching and batting in every available space.

Volleyball: The year was 1917, and the players again YMCA members, when volleyball first came to Korea. The first national exhibition games were played in 1925. Koreans took to this lively sport with special enthusiasm, possibly in part because the playing space was constricted compared with that needed for most team sports, and it was thus easier to set up games. In the Montreal Olympics of 1976, the Korean women's team captured the bronze medal. The following year, Korean girls were the champion in the First World Junior Volleyball Games in Brazil. In 1980, Korea hosted the First Asian Junior Volleyball Championships, and won gold medals in both the women's and men's divisions. Ten or more nations have invited Korean coaches to train their players.

Basketball: Basketball reached Korea as early as 1907, brought by an American enthusiast named Gillette, who was probably in Korea for some other reason that sports history does not record. The first nationwide tournaments were played in 1920, and the sport has retained its popularity among both men and women. Koreans have repeatedly taken prizes in the Asian Games, and have come to be regarded as the best basketball players in the Orient. Korean teams also took second place in the Women's World Basketball Championships in Czechoslovakia and fourth place in the World Championships in Brazil in 1971. Korea hosted the 8th World Women's Basketball Championships held in Seoul in 1979 at the newly-dedicated Sports Complex Gymnasium, with 12 teams participating. The U.S. won the gold medal, Korea the silver and Canada the bronze. In the 1984 Los Angeles Olympics Korean women won a silver medal in basketball.

Tennis: Tennis was apparently first played in Korea about 45 years ago by Seoul National University stu-

The opening ceremony of the 66th National Sports Festival was held in the Olympic Stadium on June 18, 1986 (top); the National Track and Field Championships were held in

the Seoul Sports Complex on May 12, 1985 (left); and Korea played Argentina on June 3, 1986 in the first round of the World Cup Soccer Championships in Mexico.

dents, but it was only in 1971 that the first public courts opened in Seoul. Since then, interest in the sport has mushroomed, among women and older people as well as youths. There are now over 360 private tennis clubs in Seoul alone, not counting commercial courts set up for profit. As for international competition, Korea's women players won gold medals in the 1978 and 1982 Asian Games.

Table Tennis: Fast and keenly competitive, table tennis has attracted Koreans since the 1920s. In 1973 the Korean girls' team won the World Table Tennis Championships in Yugoslavia, and three times in a row, in 1975, 1977 and 1981, advanced to the finals. In 1980, Korea inaugurated the Seoul Open International Table Tennis Championships, which has turned out to be one of the largest in open table tennis history.

Golf: Until as recently as the turn of the 1960s, the number of Korean golfers did not exceed a thousand. Now there are an estimated 1,300,000 golfers and the number is expected to grow steadily with improvements in the standard of living. There are 26 golf courses in Korea, mostly of the country-club type, managed on a membership system. Nearly all first-class clubs have a waiting list for affiliation. Seoul is the next-to-the-last leg on the Asian circuit with prize money in 1985 of US$120,000.

Archery: Archery in Korea dates back to the days of pre-history, but modern interest in the sport was stimulated when in 1978 a young Korean contestant Kim Chin-ho won a prize in the Bangkok Asian Games, and went on to take five out of six gold medals at the World Archery Championships in Berlin the following year. Since that time both the modern and traditional archery circles in Korea have been experiencing a boom in interest and participation.

Skating: Winter sports have always prospered in Korea, which has a long winter season of relatively calm weather. In South Korea, however, skating is limited to about one month when the paddy fields and shallower rivers freeze hard enough for safe skating. Still the number of skaters is ever increasing, and a rink with artificial ice and a 400-meter track has been in use since 1971. In 1976, a Korean Lee Yong-ha won the World Junior Speed Skating Championships in Italy. Korean figure skating aspirants are training rigorously for a crack at international competition in this field.

Skiing: Skiing arrived in Korea around 1920 due to the enthusiasm of an unnamed foreign missionary and today attracts around 1,000,000 participants annually. There are three major ski resort areas, all easily accessible to Seoul.

Wrestling: Both free-style and Greco-Roman wrestling became prevalent in Korea after introduction by a Korean student returned from Japan. In the 1964 Tokyo Olympics, Korea emerged with a bronze medal, while the Montreal Olympic Games in 1978 produced a gold medal in the featherweight division and the 1984 Los Angeles Olympics, two gold, one silver and four bronze medals.

Boxing: The first recorded boxing match in Korea took place in 1912, and the sport retains remarkable popularity. There is rigid division between professional and amateur boxing, each with its own association and rules. Eighteen Korean professional boxers have earned world titles since a Korean won the WBA junior middleweight title in 1966. In the Asian games, more than half of the championships are won on the average

A schoolboy learns t'aekwondo, a self-defense martial art that Koreans have developed over 2,000 years.

by Koreans, who have also won more medals in international Olympic boxing than any other category of athletes.

Shooting: Because Korea has universal military service, and a favorable terrian, marksmanship has been a natural sporting event to predominate. Korea hosted the 42nd World Shooting Championships in 1978 at the specially constructed T'aenŭng Range in eastern Seoul, the first Asian nation to sponsor this annual event. The electronic scoring system was used for the first time for the 300-meter event. During the First Asian Ladies and Junior Shooting Championships held in Seoul in September 1977, Korea won 36 of the 37 gold medals. Korea also successfully hosted the First World Airgun Shooting Championships in 1979.

Swimming: Until around 1969, interest in swimming competition was minimal in Korea. But after three Korean swimmers won gold medals in the 1970 Asian Games, there has been a rapid increase of participation, accompanied by an expansion of pool facilities of international competitive standard. From a seaside recreation indulged in by most Koreans, swimming has become in addition a focus of athletic competition.

Ssirŭm: Among several categories of traditional sports that have experienced revival in modern times, the ancient form of wrestling called *ssirŭm* is notable. Tomb murals from the Koguryŏ Kingdom demonstrate that this sport is at least 1,500 years old, and perhaps much older. Today it is popular because of the relative simplicity of its rules, being more a "fun" sport than a serious competitive form of athletics.

T'aekwondo: *T'aekwondo* is a self-defense martial art that Koreans have developed over 2,000 years. It has become a popular international sport in the last quarter century, and thousands of Korean instructors are active in gyms and institutes around the world. The *T'aekwondo* Association of Korea has a membership of 1,800,000, and the World *T'aekwondo* Federation was established in 1976 and holds semi-annual matches. Forty-seven nations participated in the Third World *T'aekwondo* Championships in Chicago in 1977, where Koreans won seven of eight divisions. *T'aekwondo* was formally recognized by the International Olympic Committee in July 1980. This is only one step short of making *t'aekwondo* a regular Olympic event, which may occur in the near future, since the number of active participants worldwide is estimated at 100 million in over 100 countries, governed regionally by five associations. It is to be an exhibition event in the 1988 Seoul Olympics.

Tourism

The flickering lights of a coastal beach town.

Korea has one of the fastest growing tourist industries in the world. In 1984, some 1,303,489 foreign visitors came to Korea, in contrast with the total of 15,184 in 1962. From being "the best-kept secret in the Orient," the nation is on its way to becoming one of the most popular places to visit in the Far East.

Nevertheless, Korea still seems off the beaten path so far as many tourists are concerned. For this reason, the individual visitor is likely to receive more personal attention from individuals or agencies catering to travelers' needs.

The country is well-equipped and able to handle efficiently all types of visitors, from the private individual to the large "package tour" group, or delegations to international conferences and conventions.

Seoul

The capital city of Seoul is a fully modern metropolis, with a population of well over nine million, boasting many Western-style hotels. English is spoken at hotel desks and in the shops, bars, and restaurants. Western food and drinks are available at numerous establishments registered with the government and designated as special tourist facilities. There are several conveniently located foreigners' commissaries where imported toiletries, tobacco, liquor and sundries are available to visitors.

Though quite up-to-date in terms of comfort and convenience, Seoul remains the repository of more than 600 years of Korean culture. Established as the nation's capital a century before Columbus discovered America, the city enshrines treasures and traditions from still earlier times. It is both a panorama and a microcosm of Korean arts and history.

Just a few steps from the major hotels in the center of town, for instance, is the Tŏksugung Palace, an example of Seoul's unique blend of the new and the old. The palace grounds are now a public park, but the buildings remain just as they were when occupied by members of the royal family. The ancient, tile-roofed throne hall, where Korea's kings once received foreign envoys, stands next to two stately Grecian-style buildings that might have come from Versailles. These were built in the early years of the century under the influence of the Westernization trend, and now house the National Museum of Modern Art.

The visitor can see priceless examples of Korea's heritage at museums scattered throughout the nation, including the National Museum of Korea located in the Kyŏngbokkung Palace grounds in Seoul: great bronze Buddhas, fantastic murals taken from ancient tombs, gold crowns, enchanting paintings, and the matchless ceramic ware famed the world over as Koryŏ celadon.

Not far away is Ch'angdŏkkung Palace, also open to the public, a much larger and entirely traditional royal residence. Its stately Oriental buildings contain mementoes of the last dynasty, including many rooms furnished just as they were when kings and their courtiers lived there. The visitor can see the royal coach and early motor cars used by the kings during the last days of the dynasty, as well as a unique blue-tiled roof and exhibits of old costumes, weapons and other artifacts. Behind the palace is the Secret Garden, a fairyland of intertwining paths linking wooded slopes, lotus ponds and pleasure pavilions.

The Korean government plans to restore the royal palaces in Seoul to their original state. The Ch'angdŏkkung has already been restored and the adjacent

A cable car ride from the foot of Namsan Mountain

up to the peak provides a panoramic view of Seoul.

Built in the 8th century, the Buddha in the Sŏkkuram Grotto Temple in Kyŏngju is known throughout the world as a pinnacle of Buddhist art (above). The stone shamanistic totem protects the village. Shamanism has been a longstanding part of Korean life.
Traditional village life comes alive in the Folk Village near Suwŏn. Here visitors may find women spinning silk thread from a small white cocoon (right).

Ch'anggyŏnggung is undergoing a large-scale restoration to be completed by 1986.

In a secluded garden across the street from Ch'angdokkung lies Chongmyo, housing the ancestral tablets of Yi Dynasty kings and their queens. It is here that one can visualize the pomp and ceremony of the Confucian-style memorial services held five times yearly during the dynasty period. Recently the ceremonies have been revived and are reenacted every year by descendants of the Yi Dynasty court family to keep alive the culture of this period. Traditional colorful clothing and musical instruments are used in this ceremony which is open to the public.

There are many other parks, palaces, museums and temples in or near Seoul. But the visitor will not wish to pass up the opportunity to do some shopping and souvenir hunting, in addition to sightseeing. This can be accomplished at one of the modern downtown department stores or arcades, or in the crowded noisy, but colorful traditional marketplaces. "Best buys" among Korean products include silk brocade, leather goods, sweaters, brassware, lacquered items and tailor-made clothes. Hand-sewn tablecloths and place settings, jewelry of gold and semiprecious stones, woven straw novelties and woolen cloth are other much-esteemed local products.

Another experience the visitor should not pass up is a Korean dinner, either at a modern restaurant or a courtly Korean-style restaurant. In addition, excellent Chinese and Japanese food is available, as well as Mexican, Italian, French and other continental cuisine.

Seoul has an active night life, with roof-top night-clubs and cabarets or tearooms perched atop most hotels and many business buildings. The best of the clubs feature good dance bands plus top vocalists and floor shows, imported liquor, and English-speaking waiters and hostesses.

For those with classical tastes, Seoul offers a variety of symphony concerts, operas and recitals, by local and visiting artists, as well as special tearooms where recorded music from huge disc collections may be played upon request.

Visitors should not pass up the opportunity to visit the National Classical Music Institute, where the ancient traditional music and dances of the royal court are still preserved and cultivated.

For a visitor with only a day or so stopover, there are perhaps two "musts" in Seoul: a visit to Seoul Tower on Namsan Mountain for a panoramic view of the city and a visit to Korea House. The latter is an old-style public mansion where Korean arts, artifacts and foods may be seen or sampled. Korean buffet luncheons, formal dinners and entertainment by Korea's Human Cultural Treasures are offered at reasonable prices. Korea House offers a chance to glimpse a "slice of life" of the old Korea.

Kanghwado Island

For a tourist wishing to take in some of Korea's pastoral beauty, Kanghwado Island is to be recommended. Situated in the estuary of the Han River north of In'chŏn Port, the fifth-largest island of Korea is rich in history and natural beauty. The road is completely paved to Chŏndŭngsa, the island's largest temple and one of the 31 major temples in Korea. The driving time from Seoul to the temple is about one and a half hours. Express bus service is also available.

The entire spectrum of Korean history, from the hazy era of Tan-gun, the legendary founder of the nation, to the opening of Korea to the Western world can be observed and studied on this island. In the 12th century Korean celadon pottery reached its highest level of artistic distinction and one of the major kilns of the era was located on Kanghwado.

Folk Village

A traditional Korean village located 30 minutes south of Seoul near Suwon reenacts the enchanting rural life in Korea hundreds of years ago. Here curious tourists might see an old gentleman with a slender bamboo pipe in hand and wearing a wide-brimmed horsehair hat strolling under the low eaves of straw-thatched homes. Or they might poke their heads into one of the many private homes. On a wood-floored porch, a woman may be ironing clothes by beating them with two clubs while in the next courtyard another housewife may be spinning silk thread from a small white cocoon simmering in a pot of boiling water.

This village was erected in 1973 and now includes aspects of almost everything uniquely Korean from days gone by. Homes typical of the various provinces of Korea can be identified. In the village square tight-rope walkers, weddings or funeral processions, kite-flying contests, and graceful dance troupes are seen regularly.

The blacksmith, carpenter, potter, and instrument craftsman can be seen at work in their shops. A *yangban* (aristocrat) house, a watermill and the neat yet humble farmer's home can be entered, and their furnishings inspected.

Pusan and vicinity

The second largest city and principal port of Korea

lies on the southern tip of the peninsula, and thus enjoys somewhat milder weather than the capital. Taking advantage of this and the coastal location, several popular bathing beaches have grown up in the suburbs of the city. The beaches at Haeundae are clean and sandy. Water is warm, currents mild, and the summer weather pleasant. Tongnae is especially noted for its natural hot spring health baths. There are several hotels meeting international standards in each town.

Just outside Pusan is the impressive U.N. Cemetery, the only one of its kind in the world, where the dead from several of the 16 Korean War allies rest in honored serenity.

Within an hour's ride of Pusan are two of the most beautifully situated and interesting Buddhist temples in the nation, Pŏmŏsa and T'ongdosa. Like almost all Korean temples, these are situated on secluded pine-forested mountain slopes, and must be reached by car or bus.

Kyŏngju Area

Perhaps the richest repository of ancient history and arts on the peninsula, the city of Kyŏngju is now only a provincial town, but was once the splendid capital of the Shilla Kingdom (57 B.C.-A.D. 935). Kyŏngju is literally a museum without walls, filled with remains of ancient Shilla: temples, royal tombs, monuments, the earliest stone observatory in Asia, pagodas, and the crumbling remains of palaces and fortresses. There is a branch of the National Museum in town where smaller and more perishable items are exhibited.

The two supreme treasures of Kyŏngju are the Pulguksa Temple, one of the most beautiful in Korea (and easily accessible, just outside the city) and the nearby

Shilla royal tombs in downtown Kyŏngju. Reflecting the cultural glory of the kingdom, temple sites, stone

pagodas and Buddhist reliefs are scattered around the vicinity of this ancient Shilla capital.

stone grotto, called Sŏkkuram, known throughout the world for the stone statues and carved friezes, considered pinnacles of Buddhist art.

Kyŏngju is highly recommended to the tourist if he has time for only one trip outside Seoul. The journey can be made by express bus, or super express train, and there is a Western-style hotel located near Pulguksa Temple itself.

Only six kilometers away, on the eastern outskirts of Kyŏngju, the government has developed the Pomun Lake Resort which is one of Asia's first-class international tourist resorts. Work began in 1974 under the Kyŏngju Tourism Development Plan as two large lakes (reservoirs) were developed in picturesque valleys surrounded by wooded mountain scenery.

The entire 2,570-acre area has two modern hotels and a leisurely atmosphere of peace and tranquility, suitable for large-scale conferences, exhibitions and other business gatherings. The lake site is not only ideally located but is also near the rich historic relics from the "golden age" of Korea's past.

East Coast Resorts

The northern stretch of Korea's east coast, which can be reached by plane, train or express bus from Seoul, is rugged and mountainous, with breathtaking scenery that has caused it to be called the "Switzerland of Asia." Skiing and other winter sports help make the area a year-round resort, but the most popular recreations are swimming in summer and mountain climbing in fall. The beaches are perhaps the finest in Korea, gently shelving into shallow water and mild currents.

The principal inland resort area is Mt. Sŏrak National Park, which boasts several Western-style lodges and hotels. There is also a beachside tourist hotel outside the port of Kangnŭng. The particularly scenic areas along the entire coastline are dotted with ancient pavilions once used for moon-viewing and wine-sipping excursions by poet-scholars of past ages.

P'anmunjŏm

Here the truce ending the fighting in the Korean War was signed, and here representatives of the U.N. and Communist sides still meet to haggle over accusations of armistice violations. P'anmunjŏm is also the site of the renewed inter-Korean contacts. It is a joint security area jointly managed by U.N. Command and North Korean guardsmen.

P'anmunjŏm is a 35-mile bus trip north of Seoul, but reservations for visits must be made a few days in advance to secure military clearance.

Chejudo Island

Korea's only island province is just an hour by jet from Seoul, but it takes the traveler to a different world. Cheju, 220 miles off the southern port of Pusan, enjoys a semitropical climate, with mild weather all year round. The plants and landscape are entirely distinct from those of the mainland, and are unique to Cheju. The beauties of the island range from lofty Mt. Hallasan, the highest mountain in South Korea, with a huge crater of an extinct volcano on its peak, to the famed woman divers who make their living garnering seafood and other marine products from the depths of the ocean, even in winter.

There are an increasing number of modern hotels scattered over Chejudo, and a highway encircles the island for sightseers.

Today's Korea is increasingly a leisure society with the

surpluses required to cultivate recreational activities like skiing.

Things to Come in Tourism

Many large-scale projects designed to develop new tourist attractions and to expand the existing ones are being carried out nationwide. The areas which are receiving concentrated development are Kyŏngju, Mt. Sŏraksan and its vicinity the Puyŏ-Kongju area, Cheju-do Island, and the Hallyŏ Waterway. These efforts are aimed at accommodating the increasing number of tourists, which is expected to reach two million in 1986.

General Tourist Information

How to Get to Korea

Information about trips to and within Korea is available free from any of the Korean diplomatic missions and branches of the Korea National Tourism Corporation abroad. Numerous travel agencies in Korea, most of them affiliated with worldwide organizations, are ready to help visitors with special itineraries to suit individual requirements.

Tourists may visit Korea for 15 days without visas, but proof of confirmed onward air reservations is required. Nationals of the following countries do not need visas provided they do not undertake remunerative activities in Korea: Greece, Mexico and Switzerland for 3 months; Austria, Bangladesh, Chile, Colombia, Costa Rica, the Dominican Republic, Liberia, Peru, Singapore and Thailand for 90 days; France and Tunisia for 30 days; Belgium, Denmark, the Federal Republic of Germany, Finland, Iceland, Italy, Lesotho, Luxembourg, the Netherlands, Norway, Portugal, Spain, Surinam, Sweden, Turkey and the United Kingdom for 60 days.

Tourists can bring in anything needed for personal

use while in Korea but must take away with them every-thing brought in. For information on longer-term visas and other inquiries, contact the nearest Korean consu-late (See list in Appendix).

Airlines

Many international airlines depart from Europe and America daily, some proceeding directly to Seoul and others connecting with Korea-bound flights at major international airports in the Far East. There are 166 flights weekly by international airlines connecting Korea with Japan, Hong Kong, Taiwan, and Thailand.

The following airlines serve Seoul on regular sched-ules: Korean Air, Air France, Japan Air Lines, North-west Airlines, China Air Lines, Cathay Pacific Airways, KLM Royal Dutch Air Lines, Kuwait Airways, Lufthansa German Air Lines, Malaysian Airline System, Thai Inter-national, Pan American World Airways, Saudi Arabian Airlines, and Singapore Airlines. The flight from Tokyo to Seoul takes only 90 minutes. Korean Air and Japan Air Lines also connect Osaka, Nagoya, and Fukuoka with Pusan, Seoul, and Chejudo Island.

Since 1963, Seoul has been included in the round-the-world air schedule approved by the International Air Transport Association (IATA). This permits any pas-senger on a round-the-world ticket to visit Korea at no additional charge.

Domestic air transport service is also provided by Korean Air, connecting Seoul with Taegu, Pusan, Kwangju, Sokch'o, Yŏsu, Chinju and Chejudo Island. Charter flights are also available.

Steamship Lines

Various steamship lines provide passenger service to Korea. Among those from the American West Coast are: Waterman Steamship, American Pioneer, Pacific Far East, Pacific Orient Express, States Marine and

Hikers enjoy the enchanting autumn foliage of reds

United States Lines.

The Pugwan Ferry plies between Pusan and Shimo-noseki, Japan, three times a week. Besides, there are cargo-passenger ships linking Japanese ports with Korea.

Railway Service

The Korean National Railroad provides super-express trains with all the latest conveniences, linking Seoul and Pusan in four and a half hours. Two express trains run daily between Seoul and Mokp'o on the southwestern tip of the peninsula.

Two types of accommodations are available: first-class and tourist. Pullman sleeping cars are attached to night express trains, and all special express trains include dining cars.

Guided Tour Services

Guided tours around Seoul and to other scenic places and historical sites are offered regularly by the Korea Tourist Bureau and other tourist services. For instance, there is a two-day tour to Kyŏngju, the

and yellows near Mt. Naejangsan in Chŏllabuk-do Province

ancient capital of the Shilla Kingdom, a Seoul half-day tour, a P'anmunjŏm tour and a Folk Village tour. There are also various longer tours such as a four-day Seoul—Chejudo Island—Pusan tour.

Currency

Korean currency is called *won*. The basic rate of conversion, subject to change by fluctuations in the market, was about 870 *won* for one US dollar as of May 1985. Currency is easily exchanged at main banks and their branches as well as major tourist hotels.

There are 1,000, 5,000 and 10,000 *won* notes and coins of 1, 5, 10, 50, 100 and 500 *won*.

Transportation Within Korea

Taxis are most convenient for travel within Seoul and are inexpensive but often hard to get. A few drivers speak English or Japanese. Buses are very cheap and frequent but crowded. Subways have been expanded in Seoul to provide for modern mass transit, while easing traffic congestion. Four subway lines, linked to subur-

White sand and surf attracts thousands to Haeundae Beach near the coastal city of Pusan.

ban electrical railroads, enable convenient trips to most major locations in and around the capital.

Rent-a-car is now available in Seoul and information about this can be obtained in hotels and tourist agencies.

For trips outside Seoul, both train service and express buses are available. Korean Air provides flights to all major cities.

Hotels

The hotels suitable for foreign tourists in Seoul are all registered with the government. Most rooms have private baths and heating and cooling systems. Facilities in most hotels include dining rooms, convention halls, bars, souvenir shops, cocktail lounges, barber and beauty shops and recreation areas. In general twin room charges range from U.S. $89.00 to U.S. $115.00 in "A" class hotels, from U.S. $24.00 to U.S. $66.00 in "B" class hotels and from U.S. $14.00 to U.S. $36.00 in "C" class hotels.

Business Hours
Most businesses are open 9-6 on weekdays and 9-1 on Saturdays. Department stores open later and close later. Small shops open early in the morning and often stay open until nearly midnight. Department stores and small shops are open on most Sundays (although many close on two Sundays or other days a month).

Restaurants
There are innumerable restaurants in addition to those operated in hotels. Many serve Western, Chinese and Japanese style food, but a real treat would be typical Korean cuisine.

Telephones
1035 is the number to dial for overseas calls and 1037 for international cables. Operators speak fairly good English. Red or green public pay phones are scattered throughout the city, and take 20 *won* for 3 minutes, after which the call will be automatically disconnected. Long-distance calls can also be made from some public phones.

Medical Service
Medical service in Korea is excellent. There are a number of hospitals staffed by professional doctors and nurses and the treatment is good. In an emergency the hotel desk will call the house physician or ambulance as required.

Civil Defense Day
Every month, on the 15th, there is an air raid drill sometime during the day, lasting approximately 30 minutes. When the siren goes off, everyone must get off the streets. An all-clear siren marks the end of the drill.

Appendices

Sŏgwip'o on the southern coast of Chejudo Island.

The National Flag

Taegŭkki

The Korean flag symbolizes much of the thought, philosophy and mysticism of the Orient. The symbol, and sometimes the flag itself, is called *Taegŭk*.

It is said that the *Taegŭk* flag was first flown in August of 1882, the 19th year of the reign of King Kojong of the Chosŏn Kingdom. A treaty was made at this time between Korea and Japan at Chemulp'o to end the hostilities resulting from Hideyoshi's invasion of Korea in 1592. To effect this treaty, Kim Ok-kyun and Pak Yŏng-hyo went to Japan as special envoys and, feeling the necessity of a national flag, originated the *Taegŭk* while on the ship to Japan. In 1883 it was formally adopted as the national flag of Korea.

The three aspects of a nation are the land, the people and the government. These are symbolized on the *Taegŭk:* the white ground represents the land, the circle represents the people, and the four sets of bars represent the government.

Depicted on the flag is a circle divided equally and in perfect balance. The upper (red) section represents the *yang* and the lower (blue) section the *ŭm,* an ancient symbol of the universe. These two opposites express the dualism of the cosmos: fire and water, day and